# Madam

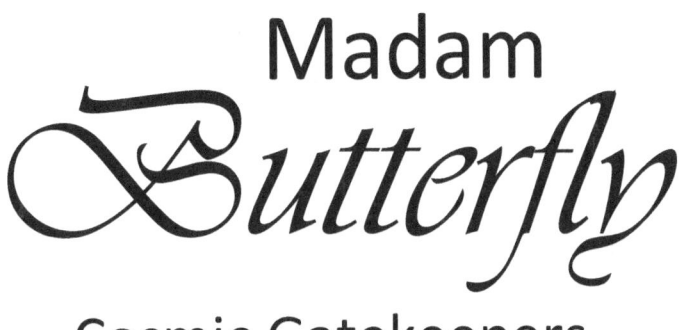

## Cosmic Gatekeepers

Monk Train Chronicle Series - 2

# Dedication

**To all Lover of Science Fiction, Fantasy and Urban Fiction**

## Disclaimer:

The written Story within this book called Madam Butterfly Cosmic Gate Keeper. Names, Characters, Places, and Incidents are the Products of the Author's Imagination, any actual Events, Locales, or Persons, Living, or dead, is coincidental.

ISBN: 978-1-7948-7926-3

Library of Congress Control Number:9781794879263

Printed by Lulu Press
www.Lulu.com/shop
www.amazon.com/books
Email: dgun7000@yahoo.com
Publisher: TwoSuns Publishing Inc.

Printed in the United States of America 2021

Another battle raging deep down thousands of miles near-earth inner core center sun hidden from human's view, Madam Butterfly never gave thought of an aliens race existing deep below the earth cradle of civilization. Just thinking only what lies above ground, not knowing perhaps that when she least expects, contacts will occur with aliens from below the earth surfaces. A sexy six feet tall blond blue-eye attractive woman never gave any clue to staff members at the natural wildlife museum, she was a superhero Shape Shifter. Collecting rare special butterflies as a hobby. If they knew she had them in her possession by law, even though she owns them, they must be turned over to the museum that employed her. On the weekends, she will go up in the Utah forest to catch stunning rare butterflies for her backdoor garden.

One particular day, she went jogging alone on the forest trails, then came upon a stranger who appears to need help lying on the ground by a falling tree. At first, she thought it was a kid because of its size, and decided to walk over toward the stranger. "Suddenly, it threw up tiny arms, do not come closer earth woman... it shouted, too many energies impulse I give off, it will make you feel uncomfortable and turn you into a butterfly." "She laughs, do you not know who I'm, they call me "Madam Butterfly?" The three feet tall alien stood looking up at her, oh, so you have two identities, I never guess in a million light-years that you look this beautiful in earth body form." "Well, let's say we keep this little-known secret between us two, she said and I can never turn into a real butterfly, that's the nickname I gave myself." "I have watch you collect butterflies over the years, you must like them?" "Oh, I love and admire them, my backyard filled with colorful ones that I have collected." "But I can bestow powers upon you to become a real butterfly if you promise to help save our planet from below the grounds you stand on from the Solar Pirates." "Ha, ha what are you talking about saving your planet below, so you are saying another world actually exit below us where I'm standing. ""Why, yes, of course, thousands of them near the epicenter of earth hot core, they are small sizes we do not spin or float." "Well, how can I fit in such a small tiny world being this size my friend, she asked?" "Come, I will show you, let us walk deep into the forest and I will bestow powers upon you to transfer you into a stunning smaller butterfly." "But I thought you were badly hurt earlier, and could not walk?' "Had to get your attention first Madam by pretending to be hurt, but I 'm ok really just need your help for my planet."

Once deep in the darkest part of the thick green forest, he flew around her at top speeds zipping through the air, with colorful flowers clings and wings attached to her body; suddenly, she shrinks smaller. "Now, floating and flapping her wings in the same spot, with her eyes still closed, ok, have the transformation occur? Do not feel any changes yet, she yelled out." "Well, open your eyes now Madam Butterfly to see the new you." "Oh, no, my body is smaller, "this is not a dream, reaching up and touching her wings, she asked; now, do I stay this way forever?"" No, no do not be afraid, this is not permeant, you can change back to your sexy blond self anytime, this will be your hidden identity." "You mean, kind of like; Jazz Man Monk Train or Superman superpowers?" "Yes, but listen carefully, you will have stealth superpowers able to go in a different dimension with plenty of weaponry in order to go into battles if needed." Now, here's the best part, you can become any size, maybe let's say up to twenty feet now that can scare the hell out of anybody." No way, museums around the world will see me as a rare species, capture and lock me behind a thick glass she said." But see, you can reduce your size and escape from them but that's for another day," "I show you, get angry about anything and watch what happen he said," Her body became sleek and stealth with shining metal protective plates increase with all types of weaponries attachments. "Go ahead try them out, he said but first, let's go into another matrix dimension that has no sounds effects, do not want to attract anyone near us." She had a ball blowing up things, shooting, and destroying all the target practice objects. "Good, so let's step back into the forest reality he said." "Damn, this is cool man, slowly she changes back into her normal self, shaking her head slightly, now I'm a superwoman." "Right, right that's another way you can look at it, it's kind of a good feeling living as a real butterfly." "I can dig this, so if I do not like the man I'm dating, I can always fly away… she laughs." "Sure, you can, but your shapeshift has limitations only in your backyard around your butterfly collection, in this forest area, and on my planet." "Remember, you do not want the museums knowing and seeing you… he laughs."" So, when you want to come down to visit, always remember to be aware that we never met or seen each other, because the sky watchers will let you fly all over the place only as a butterfly." "See, if they suspect that you as a shapeshifter could be a spy for the enemies, they will shoot you down." "Who's the Sky Watchers?" "They are flying six feet's gentle giants that guards the skies over our planet, all the forest, and love seeing pretty natural butterflies." "So, why do you hide yourself from them she asked?" "Never want any of them to see my face; once attack might have to escape back up here to convert into a butterfly-like you." "Yes, I see your point, some of them will point you out to the enemies of the planet to be captured, you will be arrested in order to stop

your movements because of your powers."
"Correct, by the way, my name is Star Seeker an explorer of future events before they occur in my world, we do not have the firepower to defend ourselves." "Guess you say; we, humans have the fire powers to destroy the entire earth." While yes, you all do, that's a man nightmare I've seen some of your battles against your enemies on the battlefield just to kill and scatters human's dreams." "Know that it's good to have a powerful large defense force on standby in order to stop aggressions if it occurs." "But a huge battle is about to take place on my planet in a few months and Neo, our gatekeeper crew does not have the elite space troopers strike forces to stop it." "Our complete existence will be wiped away, we cannot live on the surfaces because of the deadly chemtrails that will biologically destroy us unless you help." "Now, we do not need your shadow regime forces and scientific community intervention he stated." "But I know for a fact that if earth scientists discover you guys down here, they will want to display you all in zoos, carry out millions of experiments and vaccinations, she said." 'So, you understand how careful we have to be about

telling everybody, some of them will have those types of agendas too."

"But I know a professor who goes by the name; Delbert… that loves to come over to the wildlife museum for conferences and lectures about unusual things, now he could be of a great help." "He has written stories about space travel and underground fantasy worlds; he has also written books about a cyborg jazz musician that works part-time as a warrior for the alien's worlds." Now, he shapeshifts, becomes clones, and many other things in order to get the job of justice and peace done, I like him." "This amazing guy still exists today, I'm one of his biggest jazz fans." "Oh, you are talking about the cyborg Monk Train… the Jazz Man knows all about his great music, but he is too large to enter our world and stay really busy in his space travels jazz concerts." "Well, you can't just assume that he might not help, however, I know Dr. Delbert will not reveal your world, he likes to keep all his research a secret because of other writer's competitions." He mostly has his secretaries type all his manuscripts on regular typewriters to keep it from being looked at by thefts online." "Plus, now, this is between me and you, he's married but I heard he have relations with some of his female college students for grades she told him." Well, you know some humans just like on my planet, you have girls that wants things given to them free, so they will give of their body to please that man." "So, if they earn a teaching degree that way without really knowing anything, the students in her class will suffer." So, now, you are giving me a lecture on morality, yes, I can see that happen in a classroom if the teacher does not know the subjects well, it can happen to guys too, she said." "Yes, I know it can happen to some of them, I kind of had that feeling that this professor that you are talking about is a very secretive person from the way he carries himself." "Oh, it's hard to get certain things out of him writing footnotes on projects." "Carefully talk to him first Star Seeker said."

"Sudden, Madam Butterfly iPhone rings, A coworker just text saying that Monk Train band is coming to Utah in the next two weeks for a five-day jazz concert. "Look like Star Seer, we were just talking about the jazzman, he will be here soon, so if he decides to intervene, I will be there too." "Funny you just bestow all this power upon me to be kind of like a superhero like Monk Train, I think this might be quite interesting to us two together, she said." "Since you can see into the future, know where to find me then we will come down to your planet, and meet this foreign alien aggression head-on." "One more thing, well I just email my supervisor at the museum and taking a short leave off from work to fight this battle its going to take some time to do." "Will do, but remember Planet Nimble's fate lies in your hands Star Seeker said as he walks over toward the gateway into his world." "Just imagine me and Monk Train working as a team, heard the rumors about him and groupie's after-hours parties. As she stood there thinking; well, just maybe he can teach me things I do not know before we go into battle. Star Seeker turns and watches her, suddenly, he yelled out… an attack is about to strike at this moment, I see it, they are around us, run."

Madam Butterfly looked up and ran to shapeshift into a stealth butterfly." "Unexpectedly, out of nowhere, a fleet of twelve small miniature Solar Pirates ships flew over ahead at supersonic speeds near the trees. They had tracked Star Seeker to the surfaces because the chemtrail made it easy to follow his DNA codes. Star Seeker ran into the forest, turned around got on one knee, aim a special weapon quickly firing at them, soon dashes up in the air pulling them away from his friend.  Madam Butterfly converted into a stealth butterfly flew up and met the Pirates in midair. The ships followed Star Seeker and Madam Butterfly into the dense dark parts of the forest. Once in sight, they locked lasers guided missiles onto the enemy's, ships destroying every one of them quickly." "More were on their way by the thousands much larger; earth early warning defense satellites picks them up and jet fighters close by engaging them head-on." All over the forests up in the sky that day, they battle the air force jets, soon helicopters making an announcement for everybody to leave the forest immediately." Tanks, Jeeps, fill with troops embarked all over at the far end of the forest looking for the enemies.

"Star seeker flew down toward the wreckage, yes they are from Phat-Z Planet, these are space pirates' ships," "Changing quickly back to a stunning sexy blonde-haired woman standing in her tight-fitting jogging black shorts as smoke rises around her from the wreckage. "See, we now got earth involved… now, we might not need to ask Monk Train Star Seeker stated." "Well, it's like this my friend down there will be an all-out war to stop Space Pirates crew, with Monk Train we can level Planet Nimble Battlefield." "He probably can show and teach me lots about battling aliens, amongst other things." Yes, he does' have extents experiences and knowledge about battlers you can learn much by his side." "Madam Butterfly reaches down and shakes hands with Star Seeker; I'll be waiting for that call friend she said." She rushed and jumped into her car in order to get away from the battle in the sky. Star Seeker stayed above ground hidden, watching the battle as it took place. Soon, the troops and tanks with missiles came near him, he heard radio chatter about the spaceships from a distance star, As the sky began to clear off, debris seem like most of Phat-Z pirates forces were expecting a blowback like the one earth gave them, they high tale back. Fifty Helicopters flew overhead announcing that if anybody is hurt and needs assistance, we will fly you out to the nearest hospitals." Troops came in from other states, Madam Butterfly flew safely back home looking at the local news headline, earth invaded by space aliens today in Utah Forest." "Up in the forest, Star Seeker listened at the news on his earpiece." "For now, it seems like they all turned went back where they came from." "The air force spokesperson will speak now," "Fellow earth citizens, there has been an unprovoked attack on our soil from a distant star system, we have a few captured dead bodies, but they seem to be dissolving," "We have placed all of them into digit freezers storage units with thick glass protections." Next couple of months, they will be shown to the world later, once our scientists have studied them." "By the way, yes they are real aliens from another planet and flying in ships here on earth." "For thirty minutes, he talks about the attack, we have now place off limits to the citizens not to attempt to enter the forest areas." There will be a fine of ten thousand dollars or four years if violation of this order occurs, this is the federal case, warning signs will be placed all over." "Only elite earth space trooper's personals are allowed and certain private citizens that are working with us."

Distance away on Phat-Z Planet, the invaders returned, we were given a big push back by the earth forces their leader stated." We are smaller mostly aliens, only magnified ourselves larger when we are fighting earth forces. If we try to live on top, they know our existence now, we will be warring with them daily." "So, we will travel deep beneath the earth… well-hidden planets to survive, we will invade a weaker planet and take it over."

They were not so fortunate to have this interior sun dynamism, contained within their world was ten light-years away. Living down below inside the gas giant planet Jupiter up in space, they must scout out for a new planet. The Solar Pirates interplanetary system is deteriorating because of atomic warfare with its neighbors millions of years ago. Storage's plutonium isotopes drainage problems occurred from old missiles battery ships. Jupiter was having its share of hidden war battles without any earth scientist knowledge, who only saw it as a giant gas ball. The Planetary system authorities gave Phat-Z Planet one year to find another suitable home, which are be destroyed by their enemies who have gained the upper hands. Karmas has caught up with them, backed up against the walls, words spread that a planet called earth has an inter-world comparable to theirs.

Deep within depths, earth hollow crust layers exist Planet Nimble thousands of miles below surfaces. As their night, skies turned greenish-yellow, later to a dark purple orange color the magnetic argon energy zapped and sizzles around its elevated peaks. Most inter-terrestrial celestial bodies are not like a typical planet, some shaped rectangle like the state of Georgia inland space. Thousands of miles away from the second inner sun epic center of earth-orbiting inside a shell dome. Radiating, and pulsating invisible flares through filters to the alien's bodies that capture and store them. There were internal forces inside their cartilage body with no vital organs or plasm system without a Skelton frame reflex's bright natural light onto the planet and sustain other life forms. Having a three thousand years life span, after its end, reincarnating onto other planets throughout the star system. All Nimble aliens are small in status, standing only three feet in height and four to five heads attached to the lower body with different personalities. Without direct sunlight on their bodies, they look ageless. Breathing the vapors gases such as the hydrogen carbon series within earth hollow cradlers, which gives them the energy to do dimensional travel.

From a distance inside the earth, the planet looks like clusters of bright shining diamonds with no cast shadows on the grounds. The aliens are able to power up all their households' appliances, tools, and teleport anywhere on their home planet. They have total independence without relying on their leaders for any assistance.

Phat-Z Planet Leader knowing that they did not have battle forces or resources to engage all tens of thousands of underworld planets inside the belly of Jupiter, that would be suicide.

Their researchers were not able to revive their dying planet within Jupiter. The pollution became worse as time went on; the process increased when they stockpile more stolen materials. The inner binary gas suns spirits increased the flares upon their planet in order to speed up the decaying of all their weapons. Living off the backs of thousands of captured alien forces from previous battles. Their stolen gold stockpiles are depleted at this point, not able now to produce weapons and high-tech space ships. In order to maintain their dominance and power throughout Jupiter, needing this precious alloy. By adding steel reinforcement to the gold gave all their ships added protection from commander's forces bombardment.

Weeks later, a crew of Pirates field's drones reported to their leader, Commander in Ruler Zubbler. Sir, we have located a planet called Nimble with inhabitants that have natural generated lights inside their bodies and a hidden gateway direct onto the earth. "Good, good said Zubbler, our raids from that location can take us to the top surfaces in order to find more gold."

"The only thing in our way is the earth elite space troopers' forces, guardians that protects the aliens, and a woman called Madam Butterfly stated one drone." "For now, like I said after the earth attack, we will find a softer target planet to rule." A meeting took place on their battleship that fateful day to enter Nimble's system in order to get a closer view of these illuminations sources. Desperate, they came toward earth in a twelfth-dimension state to avoid detection from earth elite space trooper's satellites through the Bermuda triangle. Their mission, look for Nimble Star to live and dominate those aliens that live there.

A large fleet of Solar Pirates ships headed toward the planet with recoiling sounds in the distance. The Nimble Star empire elite space trooper's bases radar screens miles away never picked up any faint signals coming from their ships below the surface. Aboard all the Pirates ships were advanced technological satellite radar jammers. Additionally, the aliens have a weather control system that is meant to create a climatic shield to carry out their agendas. Substantial rain fell instant with a deafening thunderstorm, lighting dancing off the tips of the tallest trees that night. The twirling cold airstreams blowing, echoing wailing sounds of Nimble Aliens shrieks throughout the planet. On the eastern side, all gatekeepers on duty losing abilities to detect enemy's ships in their airspace because of the noises from the unusual lighten strikes. Their advanced elite space troopers' systems were foreign to that much drumming effect. Good at camouflage, their ships to give illusionary appearances like a chameleon they were able to convert all ships into tourist landers. The guardians never once felt the impulse from these powerful ships, after they cut down their trust engines and cruise in silence upon their prey.

Shielded by the huge mountain boulders, a gigantic dense floating forest sets high on in the sky over their metropolis, with glass top roof houses below to receive light waves. Never in millions of years have the inhabitants witness such violent storms that night, without a forewarning from their weather officials first. It affected Nimble's body lights that badly lit the inside of their surroundings. The closer the strange ships approach their cities; the dimmer their natural body light sources became. Within the close range, all Nimble's radar came to life sending out alerts warning of dangers; thousands upon thousands of guardians rushed out and surrounded the ships.

Neo, the leader of all Nimble's guardians spoke to them through telepathy, as he stood, the raindrops never touched him. Ruler Zubbler stayed aboard with all his drone guards to escape in case the alien sees through their deception. Later, the pirates exit slowly from their ship's bay area without getting a drop of water on themselves because they knew the damages caused by the lethal water droplets. All were short, having round bodies with single small heads that uses the same languages that was studied earlier by their computer systems and taught to them as they headed toward this planet. One of them spoke, "We are in search of fuel and came from a faraway place, and could we wait here until our fuel ships arrive?" Have to check with the authorities, first stated Neo, do you not have a huge mothership up there that are carrying such payload for things like this?" "No, we do not, our Astro-pilots has a computer energy gauge failure on most of the ships stating; we are low in isotopes fuels, he stated." "We do not carry that type of radioactive material here said another gatekeeper." The weather seems to have no effect on the visitors as they floated around and talked amongst themselves. A few of them wonder away from their ships in the darkness, but a large group of Nimble's guardians trailed them at a distance.

As the storm let up, the Solar Pirates upon noticing two adults lying on the street. "They rush over toward them, "get back yelled the guardians, and help is on the way, one of them yelled." The brilliant lights glowing from their transparent bodies were getting fainters by the minute. "We have a physician amongst us let him help these poor dying aliens! One Pirates bellowed out." They leaned over the limped bodies; check for energy pulse to stabilize their lights beam stated the physician. Ten minutes later, "Stand back, please! Here's help now said one of the guardians." Looking around in the darkness, the other pirate's earpiece device picked up sounds of a woman moaning, it was two adults having sex by a building within feet's from where they stood. Slowly, they eased away from the sight laughing; let them reproduce more aliens for us to rule. The rescue workers with their GPS computers guided them to more dead bodies. Now, this is a good time to snatch these Nimble's bodies into our shrank devices one of them said. As they floated around zapping up as many as they could, then rushes back to the scenes to get more bodies. They knew from espionage campaigns that Planet

Nimble Star has no massive missiles network defense systems like earth forces, relying solely on the gatekeepers to protect their world.

Nevertheless, all the aliens retain bits of knowledge and information's through their twenty sensory body systems. Whatever computer functions they have on Nimble; they can do it with their minds faster, that's what frightens the Solar Pirates Leadership.

Life went on inside the Chief's Vessel as they set and wait for the fuel cargo ships to arrive. When I step feet on this planet again, all shall be under my control he stated to one of his councils. Sir, we must remain cautious about what is being discussed, they could be aboard in another dimension observing us. "Ruler Zubbler glances around the space ship interior, whispers to his guards, turn on the anti-protected intrusion shields now." As the shields went down, ten guardians tried to escape and was frozen in their tracks. "What shall we do with them Chief, asked one of his drone guards." "Another council intervened, let's show compassion this time and release them back to their kind." "Who's running things around here Ruler

Zubbler snapped at the council?" "Of course, you do sir, but in order to make our stay comforter and keep their guards down, please get rid of them now." Let me think about it, ok, ok let them go he shouted out again to the drone's guards. As the shield lifted, all five gatekeepers stood up as though nothing ever happened, continuing to look around the ship interiors. Now, all the landed ships sent a code symbol of silence, only talk about pleasant things during the rest of their stay.

Now, their two light-years journey to this planet were paying off. The Solar Pirates wants to gain more insights on the Intern bright light energy inside the Nimble's transparent elongated bodies.' This gives them tremendous power at only three feet in height, with four to five colorful heads attached, they speak mostly in echoing language sounds, while a particular gatekeeper, Neo speaks many languages beyond their planet. The Pirates wanted to take over the complete Nimble Star and use their gateway to invade earth and steal all its gold too. Knowing that the blame would be on the planet's inhabitants for generations to come, earth forces would follow them and strike at the Nimble's homeland first.

This will give them a chance to high tail back to their planet without a scratch on their ships. Built the ultimate weapon, to back all their enemies up on Jupiter to a standoff, rebuilt Phat-Z Planet up. They knew from eavesdropping that Neo was the right alien and most intelligent vanguard an eye kept on him at all times. As Ruler Zubbler stares thoughtfully, his ship without windows at Neo without saying a word, afraid the Nimble's spies inside would know their plans. Knowing that he must be dealt with swiftly by having the only key to reach either world. Finally, the Solar Pirate fuel ships arrive after a week on Planet Nimble. Thanking them for their stay, the rest of the Pirates boarded their golden shining ships and headed back home to Phat-Z Planet.

A day later in Solar Pirates kingdom, a meeting was held again on the occupation of Nimble Star Planet. Ruler Zubbler stood before his comrades. Look, we have their natural system in hands now. Our engineers and scientists have studied the light source coming from them and create a cloned artificial one from it. Their natural light will be replaced with special materials that grows inside their bodies. However, we need to build artificial suns to live under, set up hidden factories up on the floating forest.

Drones Guards has dropped off all captured Nimble Aliens back into their floating Lost Forest. From our mothership orbiting above the earth, we will send many elite space troopers Pirates as tourists on trips every month in order to check its progress. I have given orders not to do any electronic communication but only give verbal reports when they return home and no one suspects anything wrong.

Therefore, the best way to win over their hearts for the take down is to play nicest. We return in large groups to Nimble Star as traders and tourists. Convincing many aliens to wear these new unique outfits of lights with two thousand built-in designs, since their natural lights bodies has only one permanent design, our goal is to, convince them that ours are better. The Nimble Star trendsetters had no problem wearing the outfits and their friends. Over time, the body material absorbs all the natural lights, making them weaker without them knowing. We will use a huge cargo ship to put their capture natural light into weaker ones by putting in charge of the ones who resist us, they will never trust each other. First, we must stop their gatekeeper and our solution be solved. See, we have enough natural light material from Nimble Star to make digital collars that would zap the gatekeeper energies. Never would they be able to embark on a dimensional journey with it locked around their necks. We would be the only one with the electronic keys our scientists have developed. Zubbler talked for the next hour on this takeover of Nimble Star. Another elite earth space trooper's commander came up to speak, all that was said a few minutes ago could work for all our goods, but we have to have a backup plan. Once we take control, we will declare a medical fake virus condition that has spread over the entire planet. "Now, our aim is that, we, the Solar Pirates will be taking the fake water down vaccines in front of them just to pretend that we have fear for these viruses. "But we give some of the water vax to the good nimble aliens that will love us and obey us to keep them alive for our good." "This will convince the rest to beg us to give it to them; we will switch to the poisonous dosages, let their own medical staff give it to them so as to see that our hands stay clear "See, they all will dare to question us since we are trying to save their lives." "Everybody laugh and gave out a roaring sound as if they were at a sports event." "This will rid the militant's ones; the main ones that will cause us future problems the vaccines will give them all type of illness within six months." "Our problem solved, and they are gone forever" "Supposed they resist taking these vaccines sir, a Pirate asked?" "Well, we will raid their homes at night for illegal drugs, kidnap those individuals and isolate them in holding facilities; brutally, forcefully put the poisonous vaccines into their arms." "Ok, that is enough for today, we will set up this operation as soon as we do a census head count report in order to see how large their population are." "Then, we divide them, up and set up vax centers all over to carry out our agenda." "Before all this occurs, let's prep first, few of us will go to their outdoors large events set up a display of viruses pictures talking mostly to the youth about how dangerous they are." "Some of you will pretend that you have the same faith as Nimble's, go knocking on their doors just to talk to them about their salvations, now most of them will have fear and take the vax. As Star Seeker listens, seeing exactly what the scheme the visitors want to do, contacting Madam Butterfly now might be too late. "Now, fellow Pirates make sure all our women reproduce a lot more pirates each month, if they have to mate with the Planet Nimble males said the Ruler."

A Solar Pirates spotted Star Seeker setting amongst them hidden in a corner at the meeting. They try forcing him to surrender, running out of the building as swiftly as he could in order to get to the portal entrance way on top of the earth. More guards zapped at him with weapons an electronic cell bar had him pinned down and all his abilities shut down. Helpless on how he will be able to contact his warrior earthly friends? "Buddy, you are through, you can get help from your friends up on the earth, well it's too late the Pirate commander told him." "In this state, you cannot send out know signal to anyone, unless it comes through me first." Since you are a very nosey Nimble alien, personally, I will make sure

you get the first dosages of the vax he laughs."
"Yes, this will cut down their growth and
lifespan of two thousand years old, the vax will
give those one's diseases and sickness too."
"This will change your DNA to keep you from
seeing into the future and soon, you will just be
standing in line, getting your meds like the rest,
take him away"

Nimble has no direct sunlight or moon; the
alien's transparent bodies gave off the lights in
the chest area that illuminates the small planet.
Once most of the Nimble Aliens take, a rest
inside their homes, darkness takes place. Ruler
Zubbler and his Solar Pirates decided to invade
in the darkness that night without any weather
devices this time. They are functioning at half
their energy levels, not able to teleport to work
or visit relatives on distant planets. By having
all their central governor and command systems
jammed, they were easy targets for an invader
such as the clever Solar Pirates. They work at
their crafts of outwitting small planets on a daily
base, finding their weakest and move in on
them. With the gatekeepers sometimes traveling
to many dimensions, they become tired and
sleepy. The Solar Sky Watchers has already

spied and studied their sleep habits years ago. The majority were caught off guard relaxing in the safe zones of their portal doorway. They slip in on their ships and place the electronic collar on each gatekeeper's neck that rested in the safety zones. Most of them were captured and placed on prison ships with all their powers and communications turned off. Few escaped this entrapment and fought back hard to no avail but were later captured, Neo battles them with lasers zaps devices, going in out of dimensions until all his energy depleted. He places his weapon back on his shoulder, and went into hiding underneath the floating Lost Forests of trees that were in midair over the city. As the Forest moved closer to the Pirates staging area, he manages to slip over by a huge tree root in order to hide fearfully of them spotting him. All over the air space of Nimble Star Solar Pirates, elite space troopers followed in and brought everybody under its control that crucial night. Nimble Aliens command forces pulled back and went to another dimensional planet to regroup. The Pirates released radioactive Isotope's flare bombs, in which, the Nimble's could not function under.

Already weak from their artificial light attachment, the elite space troopers decide to surrender to spare lives. Seeing this, he turned invisible, swirling around at one hundred sixty-five miles a second, converting into light energy, Neo making a quick dash up through the portal escape route into the dense forest of Utah. The portal entrance was very quickly filled with a solid clear substance that cause their ships to lose power and control, with that, it blocked the invaders.

A few days later, cautiously walking around in the Utah dense forest, Neo exposes his body to the earth's bright sun in order to receive more radiation to create a clone of himself. He stayed well hidden from all the troops and air force personals in the forest. After the final stages, please with what stood before him, they sit around and talk about the Solar Pirates invasion. You will go back down to Nimble, pretending a total surrender to the enemy. Neo glances at him, wondering while his head is down and a sense of sadness on his face. "This is our future, the pirate invaders must be destroyed the clone put on a great show off in the forest" "He flew invisibly through the thick trees to avoid earth elite space troopers, spoke many languages, etc. Neo stood there proud at the achievement that his twin self-had accomplished in mere few hours that day. Slowly, it lifted its head, and spoke exactly the same thoughts and words that came out of Neo's mouth. I see, we have almost the same powers; you sure could have fooled me if I saw you somewhere else, but let us see how the enemies react. "This way, if they capture you, the clone, they would not have the original Neo." "Yes, you are right, without the original you, I cannot exit as you, but of course, you can make more of me from you."

He would remain here in the forest to slowly regain his energy back from creating the clone and contemplate Nimble Star's future. Standing there, as the clone stares at him without saying a word, they shook hands and departed. As the cloned Neo enters back into Nimble Star, Solar Sky watchers immediately surrounded him with cautious weapons drawn." "Look! Chief, he decided to turn himself in, this could be a trick, one of a now traitor Nimble Sky-Watcher stated." "Now, Neo sees the very aliens he been living amongst and guarding have turned on him to save their hides. Thinking, really have to get this mess to straighten out, and sooner the better.

Ruler Zubbler stood and stares at Neo's clone, knowing that fighting spirit was still in him. The clone Neo convincing Zubbler to let him continue his duties. "We will put certain restrictions on you and the rest of the gatekeepers that we have captured." "You may continue all of your duties Neo, that is your make up and remember always that I am in charge now." "To make sure you all stay loyal to my leadership, I added my own Sky Watchers to yours to monitor every transformation, then he laughs." Go before I change my mind and have you put to death. As the clone flew around the planet, sending a cryptic signal back up to Neo. Noticing not all citizens were under their control, letting some keep their natural lights and serve the enemy. The only things left to do now is for me to fall in line like the rest and help keep the Nimble World going forward, the drone thought.

Soon, he notices that Star Seeker was captured and was calling out for help in an electronic cell, not able to flee. After hearing Star Seeker's entire story about going up to earth and contact Madam Butterfly, she will know what to do. Neo knew he had to pass this message back up to his real self. "Know talking to the prisoners a Pirate Guard looked and yelled loudly." Somehow, they have modified the skies all over Nimble to stop all types of shifts changing and communications with chemtrails. Not able to go into an invisible mode and get to the portal entranceway back up to earth surfaces, now stuck below. A way must be founded, he thought.

Meanwhile, back up on earth inside a huge underground hidden damp cave, the real Neo stood in silence for a second. Moments later, he heard familiar voices of the Nimble that has decided to ascend above the forest. At high speeds, like a shooting star with a blazing tale he flew around the forest that night in an invisible mode in order to avoid detections. Not able to slow down, gazing at their hollow imprison faces trapped inside the forest leaves. Knowing how both of their destinies were tied together. Nothing he could have done to stop this takeover of Nimble Star Planet from their enemy, the Solar Pirates. Now, most of the gatekeepers are captured and in isolation away from Nimble's Star System replace with Pirates.

Neo clone and the rest of the Nimble Aliens below the forest grounds have to solve this problem, ridding the invader from their land. How they manage to invade without using any destructive weapons of any kind taking the alien's natural light sources gradually away from them.

Going back into the deep cave dwelling to find refuge from the earth's climate and out of sight from the elite space troopers. He reclined under a large rock open and fell asleep as the rainstorm continues; it sets on a high cliff facing away from the forest. This made it hard for anyone to spot him.

Morning arose, sunshine rays of lights glimpse from behind the heavy dark gray clouds, as he makes his way through the undergrowth thick pathway. Pausing for a moment, I cannot continue nourishing off-earth oxygen, to pollute for my body cannot survive here too long. Struggling to walk the pathway and falling, he laid unconscious on the ground near the Nimble Star portal exit to earth. The next day, he awoke from the heat of the sun on his face, uh look like I have been here all night. This warmest gave him an energy boost to stand up. From the first day, he came here weak it stayed cloudy, now he welcomes the sun. Must go back up to the hidden cave off the cliff area before someone sees me.

"As he looked around, a beautiful butterfly flew by, saying you must leave this area now friend. "Why should I, you must work with the Solar Forces, he snapped!" No, I do not, there are human nature students from the Utah University who climb these rocks and walks these trails about to enter where we are in a few minutes." "The earth elite space troopers escorting them around, in case we get invaded again. "Follow me, I will show you an escape route we all uses and you will be safe there." Neo trustily follows his new friend with caution, a moment later, back in the cave now, he is out of the danger zones.

He walked underneath the forest's thick roots and vines pathway getting a small amount of sunlight that penetrates through its cracks. Realizing this might be permeant, to live out the rest of his life from being a gatekeeper in isolation from Nimble Star. Lying on his back staring up at the animals running overhead like a congested freeway in a large city. Well, hidden from them, knowing that he could be their feast if caught. Only a little bit of the sunlight feeds his body through the vine's cracks, giving it some nourishment. As he eased from the underground trail of thick vines and climb to the surface. Turning in all different direction making sure no wildlife threats was near this time.

"You are safer to move around in the evening when the sun goes down," a familiar voice said to him again, and it was his friend the butterfly." "Seems like you know your way around here pretty well said Neo" as he walks toward the forest edges cautiously watching the troops. "Sure, I do say the butterfly, just want to make sure all visitors in the forest are safe to enjoy their stay. "What do they call you asked Neo?" Madam Butterfly she said, "I escaped, and remained here after a group of students capture most of my friends in nets for class studies after overhearing them talk." "See, we have something in common, must stick together he told her, so she must be the one Star Seeker told me to contact." "I watch your back and you watch mine Madam Butterfly stated." "Sure, he said, thinking must I trust telling her now what going on below. He walks stood behind a huge boulder jetting up out the ground, making sure no one sees him." "Coast clear again said the butterfly." "Glancing down at a small town in the distance, wondering what life is like there?" "Many humans, buildings are down there she said, you are much safe up here." For a little while, my body cannot take earth pollution, can you do me a favor? "Depend on what you want me to do stated Mama Butterfly." "Have you ever been down to Planet Nimble through its portal way?" Ha, ha many times, I have a few friends I visit every now and then, oh yes a cool place, so what do you want me to do?" "We have been attacked by my Solar Pirate Alien Forces and I need to get in contact with my other self, in other words, a clone of me." "No problem, so I just go find someone who looks and has your name." "But you must be very cautious, they have seeded the air space all over, bring back any message he gives you."

Suddenly, Mama Butterfly smiles, now I will help Star Seeker for them to disappears through the portal entranceway down toward Planet Nimble for the first time. Flying high above the seeded dark clouds and spotted Neo clone. All the large sky watchers just waving at her, a harmless beautiful butterfly.

Scanning the entire areas to the floating forest, with no guard's insight, she flew down near Neo. He took notice of all the pretty colors and smiles on her face. "Seems like I brought a happy smile to someone today Mama Butterfly said in a happy voice." "You are not working with them, the clone Neo asked, as he glance around to make sure this was not a trap." "No, I spotted you miles away, you look just like the real Neo upon earth in the forest." "I am on your side and your other better half back up in the forest of Utah wants information's and I will deliver it to him." "How can I trust you? You might stab me in the back, he said." "Well, it's like this buddy, you get to compete or get wiped out by these Pirates or give me what I came for, the choice is yours." "After telling her what Star Seeker told him to get in contact with Madam Butterfly, she will know what to do." "You are talking to her now she said." "This cannot be you, look at you, small and frail they can just clip your wings and you are done he said." "Look, do not let my outer appearance impress you the wrong way, I can lay it down thick catch my drift, plus I 'm not down here to be judge." "Ok, you win Madam, most of my powers have been zapped up by the enemies." "So, explains to Monk Train about our plight down here and needs to get him involve, do not need earth shadow regime forces involved."

After returning to the surface and relaying all the info to Neo, they set out to find this cyborg jazz musician Monk Train. They went back to the edge of the forest, stood behind trees away from the troops; Neo notice the same person permitted by the authorities who always jogs along has a strong aura around him. He will stop using his iPhone recorder talking into it to write about the space invasion that took place here a couple of months ago. As he jogs higher into the forest, his aura becomes a bright emitting light, the more he studies this human-made him wanting to get to know him, but not now.

As time flees, Neo would lay below the trees thick roots hidden underground, knowing in this state of mind would not serve him well. Every day in the afternoon, his friend this time jog by with an entire group of people, they all had energized bright lights aura spewing from their bodies. Neo jog behind all of them in the fifth-dimension state that day, fully charged up, and excited. He started doing backflips, cartwheels, and flew to the edge of the earth's ionosphere in seconds. Thinking, I can safely be united with them, they are the only ones passing through here that have a powerful aura. It would be impossible to remove their sun and take it to Nimble Star Planet. They and many more along with the forest will have to go toward their second sun in the center of the earth to survive. Nimble Star cannot get that much energy from the sun in the center to regain its full strength. They need the one that shines on earth to zap back and remove the invaders. For few days, he and his new butterfly friend watched this group go jogging by, rest of the folks that runs by has a small amount of aura white light. Suddenly, she saw Dr Delbert jogging by pretending not to know him, because he must never know me as a simple butterfly as she looks over at Neo. I will just let the two meets on their own terms, so, when Monk Train arrives on Thursday, I can go over details about the invasion with him. "See you later, Neo Madam Butterfly said and flew away."

Neo thinking maybe, just maybe, I can convince him to help restore energy back to Nimble Citizens… he thought. How will I trust him? their scientists might want to study and then slowly depopulate the Nimble population. As he ran closely behind him reading his mind, noticing the person a scientist and professor of mathematics. Neo would stand at night on the edge of the forest easy picking out the scientist's home in the distance, because it glows much brighter at night.

I hope they would not be frightened of me if I approach him. He has four legs attached to his elongated torso, four arms, and a dog-like face. Being four feet in height and weighing only seventy-five pounds, gave him the advantage to hide from dangers. Never need food to eat, lives off energy boosters in the air. Super intelligent to speak all the language throughout the universe.

As the professor pass him all along this time, Neo transform into a fifth-dimension entity and ran right beside him in an invisible mode.

Once inside his home that evening, he noticed his brunette wife Cindy and five kids were meditating in a room. Staying invisible, the entire time not letting anyone know a stranger was lurking amongst him or her. Somehow, the two Maltese dogs sense his present but never bark just wagged their tales, but kept a keen eye on him. Once he found out Dr. Delbert's name, convincing himself this could be the answer to saving Nimble Star. Star Seeker never informed Neo that he has already met and talked with Madam Butterfly to help save them, in case they get attacked. He knew the plots behind the takeover of Planet Nimble Star as a staging ground to invade earth and take all its raw iron resources. Must figure out a way to approach him, a clever plot was put into play.

As Neo jogged that day and transform his body into a medium-size rock in the middle of the trail. Dr. Delbert and his two dogs came jogging by, he slowed down, notice a glowing rock on the ground surfaces. They were near a large lake of water... three miles from any of the troops where they slept, batteries of missiles on launchers sets all around the lake. This time, the two dogs never barked again, they went over to sniff and lick the rock. He reaches down to remove it from the trail, suddenly, he heard a weak voice calling out for help. He stood there for a second noting that the rock was moving in and out of dimensions. "Come back over here he called out to his dogs, taking out his iPhone, about to call an ambulance. "A loud piercing sound emitted from Neo "Stop! Do not call them, my world would be destroyed!" With a concerned look on his face, Dr. Delbert blurted aloud, "Who are you, how do I know you can be trusted, he asked?" Abruptly, a few earths elite space troopers helicopter flew over them; they knew the professor has permission to be in that area waving at him. The dogs started barking because of the frightening loud noises and all the forest animals went into hiding.

Must think of something fast to say before he has those authorizes landing, he thought. "Neo, recoil from the rock, saying Professor Delbert do you remember the planetary experiment that gave you lots of problems in college." "Why yes, that was a few years ago, what has that got to do with you?" "It was I that came into your dreams and put the answers into your subconscious mind, stated Neo." "I recalled getting most of my complex answers through dreams, and you want to take all credit, shame on you sir?" I do not have entities from other worlds living inside of me he stated. We all have past life's prehistoric generations living as spirits inside all creatures. "So, now, I'm a creature, how will my family deal with me, he asked?" The question now again, how does you know I'm a professor he asked Neo?"

Suddenly, Neo stretched out both arms and flew into the sky like a fierce rocket ship, returning within split seconds, convinced now, he asked him?" "The dogs now wimping, looking up at the Professor as he scratches his head removed his eyeglasses. "Now, what you have just done my friend defies gravity on earth, now we have lots to talk about, stranger." "However, before I can accept you into my home, I must scan you for radiation on this iPhone counter device." "Anybody that travels that swift outside a structural container must contain a high number of radiations, then land back in one second." "Where is your spaceship and what star system are you from, pal, the Professor asked him?" "I'm Neo, from Nimble Star inside the earth, where you are standing, he said." "I just knew you were going to say something like that, they really drop you off and went back up in space the Professor stated." "As he gazes at Neo face seeing how puzzled he was, just joking friend, well you already know my name, and welcome to earth Neo, my intergalactic pal, as he smiles."

"Now, you must make me a promise not to let the elite earth space troopers or any outside groups know about my existence, stated Neo?" "I have a friend up in New York that's a cyborg jazz musician name Monk Train and I know he should know about your plight," "So, this is where the rubber meets the road, yes, yes, Mr. Monk Train… I heard of him; I will definitely need to talk with him." "So, you heard about the prophet that fights all galactic evil, Professor asked?" "While, yes, I have, Neo yelled out with excitement!" "You have my words on that pal, with your permission, I will contact Monk direct." "He will work behind the scenes and help solve Planet Nimble's biggest problems." "Would that be ok with you, outsiders would never know a thing about our meeting, it's a total secret with me, the Professor asked?" "You are correct said Neo, with an amuse look on his face."

On a Tuesday afternoon, Professor Dilbert was home from work, relax, and ate dinner, later went into his study room. There, was his friend sitting on the floor over by the window gazing up at the forest. "What do you like to eat pal, asked the Professor?" "Like the cold blood mammals, you have in the oceans I only intake invisible creatures from air molecules, he stated." "Mean to tell me you can put burger King out of business, oh just another joke." This is getting very deep, here, I got a guest from a distant star system that lives off our chemtrail polluted air, he thought. "Yes, it is laden with chemicals, must get back home soon before I mutate to look like you, just joking Neo said." Pointing at Neo, how do you know I was thinking those thoughts he asked?' "On earth, you called it telepathy for someone to read your mind, it's natural for me, said Neo." Dr Delbert knew secretly he had a jewel of the universe living in his home that is the way it's going to be. "I see you have a good hobby as a musician Dr. stated Neo." "Well, if you call it that, my friends and I have a little group band to let off steam on the weekends." Neo raised his left hand; the keyboard came on automatic and beautiful chords came from it. Looking amazing at his new friend. I contacted Monk Train, but he is on tour seven light-years away and won't be back for a whole month. He did send back a clone of himself to hold things down until he return home. But you know a clone is different from the original Professor stated" Yes, I do know Neo said, the original persons have a direct communication line with the creator of the universe, a clone just imitates and pretends. The Monk clone will give a jazz concert here soon to play down his meet us up near the portal entranceway to your world.

The average earth person would never guess in a million century that Neo a vanguard to hidden worlds stays with Dr. Delbert. When his kids goes to school and his wife attends an annual meeting on boards of certain corporate, the whole house becomes Neo haven. This way,

Neo would slip into their sunroom and get all the natural sunlight energy on earth to be able to regain all his energy fully. For now, the Professor's family knew nothing of his out-of-this-world friend, Neo, except their two dogs, they are not going to talk.

The only way to get the brilliant natural lights back to all the Nimble Star aliens, Dr. Delbert and Monk clone have to play a part. They would be the bridge, letting the earth-sun magnetic beams travel through their bodies at light speed. Nimble Star citizens that still have their natural light would telepathically receive energy waves from the earth. The two would soar high above them fully charge and send beams down to them. The enemy has not figured out all of the traditional secrets about Nimble Star forbidden dimensions layers, only they can enter this place. Monk must be the one to bring new lifeblood to your planet, Professor Gilbert stated. This way, the Pirates Sky watcher can never enter, the energy mostly from Monk has good karma and can be poured into the weaker Nimble citizens. Most of their minds have been altered after this takeover, because the enemy has transferred their negative thoughts into most, except the strong-minded ones for domination control. With this method, many of them will regain their original minds and automatic come back online, and slowly turn on the pirates and their leader Zubbler.

The regular Nimble Star Sky Watchers under Ruler Zubbler commands help keep under control their own citizens and me, not knowing that I am a drone of Neo. The Sky Watchers will soon team back up with Monk train and find the prison planet to free the other gatekeepers. After this is over, we will put safety measures into place to stop any future aggression from occurring. This earth energizer outside force would cause the Solar Pirates to fall from grace. They have the power of controlling all gatekeepers with a special collar for now. On earth, the sun's magnetic energy in the shady forest gives Neo more power to do whatever he wants. Sometimes, on cloudy days, he would fly above the forest and get a direct point of contact with the sun energies, to get supercharge faster.

As Monk Train, concert ship landed at the Utah Universe Spaceport, the security forces exit first, soon Monk follows as cheers goes up and hands clapping. Madam Butterfly was standing amongst the fan, remember meeting him once backstage at a concert-signing autograph. Now, she has developed into a stunningly sexy woman, thinking of how she can approach him now to talk about helping to save Planet Nimble. "Maybe, I can attract him to me with this sexy outfit I' am wearing, but she saw plenty of sexy girls' groupies half-naked reaching at him, as the bodyguards pushes them back. No, I just go to his concert tonight and get my autograph at end of the concert, smiling walking away.

That night, the concert was kicking at the entertainment Center, for some reason, another attractive girl was reading poetry. Saw in the papers Monk Train and Octavia had gotten a divorce after five years of marriage, could not deal with those female groupies. Always promise he will stop making out with some of them, he never did, so she had enough of his promising.

During a break, Madam Butterfly struts her fine sexy self near Monk Train as he stood talking to a friend, from one corner of her eyes, she saw him glancing her way. She smiles and waves, he winks and kept talking to more fans, signing autographs. I am going to wait until after the jazz concert to get mine signed, she thought and walks back to her seat. "Sure, enough there she was in front of the one and only the jazzman himself Monk Train." "I see you like my jazz music he told her, here's a special ticket pass to my private after-party do not be late he grins and signs his autograph."

By 2 a.m., most of the party crowds has left. Madam Butterfly hung around setting in a chair chatting with a friend on her iPhone. Security came over; miss the party over in fortune you will have to leave now. Monk Train looks over spotted her she's a shapeshifter, thinking that's the same pretty woman I saw early today, he walks over. "Ha, fellows this is one of my close friends she has some personal info to give me." They stepped back and walks away; they knew he wanted to be with her. "Monk looks at Madam and asks where her date is, told him I came alone and could I have dance and I will be on my way home." A slow song came on, now she can show him what she is working with. With both arms up around his neck, his large arms tightly around her waist she started grinding all up on him. "Girl, what are you trying to do to me he asked?" "Well, it's like this as one of your favorite jazzes fans, I have fantasy about you and I together many sleepless nights all bye my little blond self, knowing you are a busy man." "He reaches down kisses her soft lips and looked into her tender blue eyes, kind late for a beautiful girl like you to be out on the road tonight all alone he said." "You know those space invaders might abduct you, then I will have to come recuse you and kick their butts." "I suppose you're right; I can just crash here on the sofa if you do not mind, so you can get your rest for your tomorrow night jazz concert." "Look, don't say another word, he grabs up a do not disturb sign, opens and hung it on the hotel suites outside doorknob. "told his bodyguards he will be expecting VIP visitors after 1:30 that evening. I looked down below his waistline saw that he was hung pretty well, now you knew I was in for a good treat tonight, have heard the rumors.

"Look, he said let us cut through the chase it's a reason we are meeting like this; we know we want each other, what do you say?" I reached up toward his tall frame gave him a wet tongue kiss for a few minutes to let him know I was ready to fu*ck. "See, you a good mine reader she teased him." "Soon, we both grabs each other hands and walks toward the bedroom kissing some more and we both wasting no time getting undress." "With his large strong arms, he picks Madam Butterfly's sexy nude body up and gently placing her between the silks white warm sheets. "Better get some of that lubricant jell over on the countertop he suggested." "Once she saw what he working with, now exciting and horny she softy rub the lubricant on him." "Thinking dam, he might not make it inside me." "Soon, she guided him slowly into her pleasure zone, started pole dance on him up and down moving in rhyme matching his every strokes." "Monk whispering in her ears baby you got some sexy skills, reached turn up the sounds of his funky jazz music on the stereo system." "Soon, she started moaning low and the sounds got louder as she hugs his neck tightly, calling out Monk's name repeatedly. Thirty minutes later, he reaches down places both large hands under her a** lifted her toward him, and slams into her pleasure zone... letting out a loud grunt sound. After taking a break without saying a word. He remounted her again; she wrapped both long legs around his waist and started wiggling slowly, hoping this feeling will never stop. Suddenly, she shaped shifts grew large colorful soft wings from her shoulders blazes that covered Monk Train back. "Screaming and moaning with pleasure as she lifted his huge frame off the bed floating all over the room." "Monk looks down at the bed, back at her, thinking dam should put her in my jazz band." He felt as if he was on a soft cloud, held onto her as she moved slowly and moaning under him." Soon, both of them let out more screams of pleasures at the same time. Two hours later, they floated back down on the bed and falls asleep in each other arms that hot night.

When the sun rose the next morning, she laid there, thinking about Planet Nimble battle and the good lovemaking she just had with the cyborg jazz musician Monk Train. Looking over at him, still sleeping; thinking I really satisfied him last night, well what can I say, you still got it girl, and smile." "By ten o'clock am, Monk stirs around looked over at Madam Butterfly, never had a blond woman throw down like you did last night baby, you are something else." "Come here, he kisses and laid it on me one more time really good and hard the way I like it." "Now, make a promise Monk right here baby why you still inside of my tight cu*t that we can get together in the future, so let me hear you say it." "Of course, baby I promise only when I visit Utah again with a music concert, see I have many fans." "Trying to make me a jealous fan Monk, I guess you are saying theirs many more sexy girls to get in line." "Monk, it's not that I want to take this relationship seriously, just want to be one of your close sexy fans for moments like this that's all." "Oh, I can dig that as he lifts and pulls her back on top of him, few minutes flew by he mounted me missionary style torn my little hot cu*t up again that morning." "Fifteen minutes later, we took a shower together; he looks in my eyes… you are a horny sexy little blond with good tight coochie, got me all horny for it." "I know it makes you feel good, and she gave him another hot wet tongue kiss." "We almost ended up back in the bedroom for round three that morning. "Let's get dress quickly baby, I won't be able to meet the music concert VIP's he said, patting me on my hot soft rump." "Might have to have you meet me again before I leave Utah Sunday night, I like the way we float around the room." "Just asked baby and I will float right back here for another special private performance." "Ok, I let my security know to let you in so here's another special pass ticket, now let me see it getting closer to lunchtime looking at his watch."

"Let's go down to the lounge for a quick breakfast and tell me more about yourself my special fan he said." Once I told him my name Madam Butterfly but left out my secret life transforming into a real butterfly, just want Monk to know me as a special jazz lover fan. Perhaps, I can surprise him the day he decided to go into battle against the Solar Pirates, he sees I 'm a fighter too she thought. Nimble problems with the takeover of Ruler Zubbler and his forces, who are willing to wages a total war to hold on to the Nimble Planet. "However, the only way to defeat them is by destroying their artificial sun making factories high up in the floating mountains guarded by large sky watchers. I will have to leave another clone of myself behind… Monk stated; by the way, I see you are a butterfly shapeshifter." "How do you come to that conclusion she asked him?" "Well, I have discerning powers being a human cyborg, when I glance your way at the Utah Space Port and winked at you, knew you were a special person and dam sexy too." "But yes, my clone can stay as long it takes to get the evil forces off Planet Nimble." "Could you leave your clone in Utah for your special fan she or maybe I can fly and meet you jokey she said with a laugh?" "Cannot stay here just to satisfy your needs baby plenty of guys here, Space Constar Umar won't allow it to happen, he laughs." "Well, that's ok, catch you when available, I see you know and read me pretty well… now I cannot pull no more surprises on you." "Now, I've heard reports that Superman Grandson carrying on family traditional maybe we can get him to tag along with us he loves to fight injustices too Monk stated." "Yes, we are three as a team can really kick some butts, bend these fools to surrender Madam Butterfly said, more the better, I'm down with that baby." She was thinking I wander can I get old Superman in a romantic grip before we go into battle, one down and another to go.

A few days later that morning before Monk Train band left Utah, Space Constar Umar delivered the clone of Monk Train deep up in the Forest area away from the troops. That day, Neo told Monk clone about the home planet Nimble Star invasion takeover, which is the main reason for his emergency plight to earth. The possibility of Madam Butterfly and Monk returning with him to bring this nightmare to end, and natural lights in the nimble aliens. Soon Madam Butterfly, Superman Grandson, what you know unexpected Spiderman came on the scene.

"Superman asked Neo why you could not let your people fly up through the portal exit in the dense Utah forest, and get their energies all at once." I am afraid it is not that easy sir, see, their bodies are all translucent, and made different from yours or mines. I have already calculated how much they need; your light level fits them perfectly. They could never survive in this earth's atmosphere, because of climate changes and intense heat from your two blazing suns, Neo stated." "So, now I fully understand my friend, you can count me in Spiderman said." Madam Butterfly casually looks over at him, well, I just put Spiderman on the backburner, I wander who told him about Nimble's problems, I thought he like dwelling in large metropolis cities around tall story buildings. "He glances over at her, whispers in a low voice near her ear; yes Madam, I like swinging from buildings and hanging upside down." "But I also like to help aliens to obtain due justice too and just love pretty sexy women with a smile." "Now, you are my kind of guy, welcome to the warrior's club she told him, see he can read my thoughts too, the girl got to be careful."

Neo is excited, ready to take on the mission with four earth superheroes that are willing to help rid them of their enemy for a good cause. He also knew if he violates the Pirates occupier's new laws and brought in strangers amongst them, his gatekeeping days would be over. Nevertheless, willing to risk it all, to free Nimble's Aliens citizens. Using the dense forest as a portal bridge to help bring his world to meet theirs with the earth elite space troopers surrounding the forest waiting on an outer space attack. He wanted everyone to receive the sun infusion of natural light from his international force's warrior. This way, Dr. Delbert can get a chance to see entirely different alien's species to write his books, and educate earth before any future fully contacts made on Nimble Star by any other strangers.

"He told all of them I love having an international warrior group for justice takes back my world from the Solar Pirates." "Now, you must find open-minded humans that can keep a top-secret about us." "Some will be the future frontrunners of a new generation that my world would interact with down the road. The people that moved here to Utah from different countries would be perfect for this too. Wherever you meet them, I shall be by your side in another dimension, picking out the positive's ones with a super bright aura. Then, I will know your colleagues can be trusted."

One of Dr. Delbert's retired nosey neighbors observed the shadow figures of Neo, Monk, Madam Butterfly, Superman, and Spiderman from the sunroom. With his x-ray, glasses Superman accidentally looked through the room wall saw across the street Professor neighbor watching and listening to them. Secretly, he sends out a high-volume frequency that irrupted the signal so he could not hear any more of their conversation and that fix him he thought. They were having a special debriefing on attacking Ruler Zubbler Pirates Forces. The neighbor finally made the eavesdropping device work again, finding out about the weird little one, Neo being an alien from under the earth deep down. His imagination running wild thinking the rest of the folks were over there plotting an outer space terrorists attack against earth one-world shadow regimes system. He never saw any of the strangers enter or leave the professor's house, wonder how this was possible until he decided to set hidden remote videoing cameras outside in his van. Twelve o'clock that night he saw four figures, and a small weird one floated from the room out of thin air, down by a streetlight they stood for a brief second and vanished again, what the hell is going on he thought! Looking back over toward the house, he saw Dr Delbert cuts off his lights in the study room, this some weird sh*t. Standing there in the window camera rolling wiping the sweat off his face cannot wait to show this to my friend's top regime people in the morning.

The next day, he contacted Joe a friend working as a supervisor in the intelligent digital network division at nearby Air Base about the dangerous information that was discussed. The outer space aliens plotting with Dr Delbert in his home to attack our nice folks in power. Once Joe viewed and listen to the video, he puts an urging top propriety on advanced technologies that needed to be investigated by A.I. Division ASAP." "Now, if all that you recorded this week is true my friend, these videos confirm a terrorist attack on our beloved one-world regime. We have a huge budget, thanks to the taxpayers, I'm going to see to it you receive one hundred twenty-five thousand dollars a month tax-free." "Now, just between you and me my friend, I want that extra twenty-five thousand cut each month, now do we have an understanding?" Well, hell yes man, never dream I can make that kind of money in a month, so each month I just go to different ATM machines and bring you cold cash how about that." "My friend you are right, we think alike now, this is only between us so do not get any wise ideas in the future, you know how we shadow regime forces operate."

Joe decided to take a personal interest in this discovery in the forest, he orders an emergency elite earth space trooper flight over the forest, dispatch a group of secret agents to follow Dr. Delbert daily. Deep space satellites with video telescopes surveillance the forest twenty-four seven and over the Professor's home. The neighbor decided to introduce himself to Dr Gilbert never letting him know what he was doing, but constants pulling information from him in a non-engaging joking matter. Not feeling bad after what he has done behind his back, but my one-world system comes first and I need my snitch reward payments he thought. At my age, who is going to hire an old seventy-five retired bioengineer man, hell he young still working over at that university. One of the students who were studying artificial intelligent robotic technologies told another student friend about seeing Dr Delbert home, him driving back and forth on Google live maps sites. So, they figure Google just had the area tied to their navigating mapping system so peoples lose in Utah could find their way around the city, no big deal.

Monk Train, Superman, Madam Butterfly, and Spiderman stood deep in the Utah forest talking to Neo away from the authorizes on standby for the invaders. They all sense they were being eavesdropped on and watched, that night superman took off went up into space found six satellites with roaming digital cameras eyes; he dematerializes went inside rewired them, and flew back down. "I see you took care of that and fixed it Spiderman stated, but my spider-sense feels they still have a target above us on the trees. "All the three of the warriors took off and flew up on top of the forest to their dismay strange heads popping out of the leaves in the Utah forest at night. From the mothership deep in Space, Constar Umar came to them in another dimension, "Monk Train, I see you have new warrior friends." "Well, Constar Umar, nice folks I might say so myself, I guess you already know about Planet Nimble turmoil." "Yes, I know all about their capture, you guys will help set them free, so welcome everyone to this platform we called justice and peace throughout the universe." "I will summon billions of Invisible Z-Drone Weather Squadrons to go up dim the two sun's rays direct." "I do not want the invaders with their artificial technologies to block the sunlight rays from any of the planets that will shorten the biological lives on all them. "We will hold an emergency meeting with The

I.S.A.F. Interplanetary Space Aliens Federation to create uncomfortable weather conditions on them to stop this madness." "Damn, Monk Train we got some heavy backup man said Spiderman." The only difference is that we only use our highly advanced weaponry for defense." "I do not see you all as Black or White just social constructs matrix traps, just one Human Race we seeded on earth Space Constar Umar stated." "And we all agree sir stated Madam Butterfly with a smile." "Superman threw his hands up, I'm down for Justice for all lives above and below the earth." "Me too says Spiderman, when we go down to Nimble help, bring Justice and peace will follow along afterward we rid the enemies." "I see all you straight-up space warriors that's good stated Space Constar Umar, as we speak your one world leader has been given wrong info." They have been informed by Dr Delbert nosey neighbor that you all are Terrorist Militants plotting to attack their shadow regime forces." He's about to send elite space troopers forces up here to try taking you four down, I won't let that happen." "You all will just be around them in another higher dimension, they want even no you are here, the

Space Constar stated then he vanishes from them."

The one world leader Orders a shadow elite earth space troops base commands branch in Utah put on high alert and standby. Intelligent field agents called to the main Airbase unit to report about what they saw close-up in the forest. Not knowing a hidden world were lurking under their feet. They were told not to alarm any of the tourist or town folks... let them continue to visit and jog in the key area only. Keeping their undercover mission secret from the entire national and local news agencies, a total blackout occurred.

Now, Neo realize Dr. Delbert neighbor snitched on them and other humans from the air force spying on the dense forest have put a tug of war between good and evil. Their mission would not be deterred or stopped by this nonsense; it must be carried out to save this world if it means having an enemy with earth forces. Local authorities became concerned about reporting echoing sounds coming from the forest at certain time a day by ordinary citizens calling in.

The shadow commands branch of the elite space troop's base in Utah had all top authorities at a special meeting. Ladies and men must inform you for safety and security of our special forces in this state, this must be kept top secret. Whenever any citizen or reporter calls in about the forest noises, pretend you are concerned, but do not dispatch any authority units up there to check. Everybody looked stunned at the commanding officer, wondering why such a harsh term; their job is to protect the citizens. You might wonder what I am saying, to be blunt, we think there are strange aliens forces up in the forest and few kindhearted earth citizens helping them. Now, we know they have not harmed anyone yet, but there is a local Professor at the junior college who somehow seems to tie an end to these creatures. We have a google mapping system tracking them, a huge ground team on him and his friends. Our Intel branches have all their entire social medias background history saving you people lots of paperwork. From this day forward, the Muti national military forces are in charge of this entire operation, any questions direct them to Sargent Harper. No communication over the airwaves or email, because our computer systems can be hacked, the State of Utah are in good hands and you can rest assure this matter would be solved quickly, thank you all for coming." The earth warrior team stood in the seven dimensions listening to all this bull crap, what a shame said Spiderman, advance in technologies but not in human relationships." Man, we all agree with you, looks like we fighting two battlefront one for Planet Nimble liberation and earth humans civilizing said, Monk." Suddenly, they all vanish from the meeting room back into the forest.

The developments that have taken place has increased the local news reporters and television station wanting to know more. Things are about to get out of hands, reporter's question the local airbase communication department about this phenomenal happen, asking about a flyover with jets. Some of the enterprising reporters flew their own drones over the area on the weekends to get a full grip of what really was going up in the forest. To mass out this noise, jazz and rock concerts were scheduled and paid by secret shadow regime branches with millions of digital dollars. Madam Butterfly had a date with

Superman at the concert that Saturday night, he invited her over to his home. "She glances around the room looking at the photos spotting Lois Lane thinking that broad went with his granddad because he has her on his walls. "He came up behind her, "glass of wine he asks with a smile." "First, where is your lady's room she asked." "Oh, upstairs to your left standing there with two glasses of wine." As she walks up the staircase noticing his bedroom door slightly close, open peeking inside saw this huge bed, hell yes, she thought excitedly and went on to the bathroom. Ten minutes later, Superman came up the stairs, over here baby Madam Butterfly yelled in a sexy voice." "He stood there with his glasses on, we cannot drink wine in the bed, not sleepy yet, he said." "Well, now take those clothes off and get in here with me baby relax lets me and you break all the rules tonight I want to tell you if you don't, she giggles." "She watches him removes his eyeglasses and clothes, be back he said." I guess right, he came right back up quickly stood near the bed with two wine glasses and the bottle. After a few drinks, he reaches over… kisses her, she just grabs him, but he flips her over on the back-mounted and had her calling his name repeatedly. When she wrapped her long legs around his back, it seems like he became more arouse and pounded away. At once, she shapes shifts, grew large wings they spread and covered superman back as she lifted him off the bed moaning. She poles dance and thrust her hips slow to give him pleasure as they floated around the room. After a few moments, they came back down to the bed, both knocked out from drinking too much wine and trying to sc**w. Madam Butterfly glances over at Superman sound asleep and the large clock that said 3 a.m., She got dressed, at least, he satisfied my needs and went on back home early that Sunday morning. Back home, she took a shower thinking Professor Delbert next on my list, Neo and Star Seeker completely out of the picture... she laughs. Do not know why I have these strong sex urges to bed these superheroes guys before I go into battle with them. Maybe they are implanting some of their DNA energy into me, feel much closer to each one now, kind of, like I really know them on the inside and outside. She got in her bed thinking maybe I dream about flying cyborgs and drones who now goes on to sleep.

Reporters stepping up their games came as tourists and moved in a house down the street to monitor all activities up in the forest. They walk their dogs by the trail, but even had no clue another world was below their feet. Neo has shift changed into an old man to keep them from being a suspect when they came around sniffing areas he has walked. He would just set invisible, glancing at them, and walks away with his head up. Reporters took to the air with more drones, used hot air balloons for tours as a cover to carry out their own assignments. The Nimble heads never appeared on the leaves when the balloons or drones flies over, because of fear.

One of the reporters took out a small hi-tech digital camera, took a picture of Neo footprints. Next few minutes, they snapped away on automatic mode. "Look one of them excitedly said! All of these images had turn out gray on the screen starting to fade. All stood in disbelief at the camera. There must be an electronic force field around this footprint. They pulled out scanners and other instruments moving up close to the unusual footprints, it disappears right before their eyes. Now panic, all rushed back to their location to have a meeting about what had just happened. We must not reveal this now to the outside world, let us gather more evidence to see where this might lead to, could be bigger than what we think so let's not jump to any conclusion yet.

Neo knew they were agents spying on the forest trail area, now he has to be very careful now. Now he has two battles to win, dealing with the earth agents, but now they all show anxiety dealing with the unknown. With that type of dreadful energy of negativity on both ends, this could be detrimental for both sides. Nevertheless, he notices they are just observing and staying back not interfering with Dr. Delbert. Maybe, they are plotting and sizing things up before, they try to intervene in our mission. The Professor caught up in an uninvited dramatic triangle about to unfold in his community. The reporters followed the special agents while they shadowed Dr. Gilbert closely. Even on his job, they watched him; never informing the college administrations staff about their investigation, fear someone might let him know, but he knew. Once he stops to pick up his dry cleaner, an agent came in behind him. As the Professor reached for his iPhone to pay, quickly glancing around and noticing the same person he saw on campus standing in line. The man grabs his iPhone pretending to answer a fake call-in order to keep himself from being recognized. Rushing back to his parked car, the agent followed and hopped into his back out quickly waiting to follow. Delbert started to back out, glancing in the rear mirror noticing the car behind, slowly he pulled back, upturns the switch off.  Setting in the car for a minute smiling, now the Dr knows he's being watched by many agents, from the corner of his eyes, seeing the angry agent just sped away.

Neo now knew the agent's leader's commander forces and Solar Pirate leader's forces would eventually clash once they try to come up on top to take earth's gold. The only thing left to do after retaking his planet back is to block the entranceway. This will prevent any Pirates from reentering Nimble Star System for a safe haven. Having no place to run or hid will end their destructive behaviors and place them within the crosshairs of earth elite space troopers' authorities.

Many neighbors became curious about all this attention now on the professor's family, one of them called up the local news station, which dispatch an investigative crew. Old doc seems to be not enjoying all this attention in a good and bad way causing him to change his daily habits.

Soon his next-door neighbors avoided speaking, placing their cars inside the garage, their kids prevented from playing with his. Same time, the agents watched from a distance, videotaping everyday Dr. Delbert home and family without the neighbors' knowledge. The snitcher across the street was really enjoying his cash money setting in a chair eating popcorn watching his large monitor with ten hidden cameras aim across the street and seeing Dr. Gilbert hounded. He will zoom in and zoom out just having a good old time all by himself. Sometimes, his friend Joe down at the elite space troopers' base will stop by on the weekends to peek and get copies for the huge files they are building up against Dr. Delbert. Thirty elite space troopers' jeeps will follow

Joe; all the guys will set outside just to intimidate the professor."

Space Constar Umar got tired of this, so he would put an invisible magnetic force field around Dr Gilbert house. His nosey became upset by not getting clear images, thinking they might stop paying him every month, got to find another way he thought. This will stop pictures taken; next, he converted all the warriors' languages into his so the agents would not understand them. "Agents decide not to approach Delbert as of yet, waiting for the right moment. Slowly reaching out in the community to see who else knew what Dr. was up too. His neighbor snitcher across the street did not want to reveal himself, comfortably paid under the table, not wanting his pictures in the news. Defying their parents some of the kids started back playing with his kids around their back yard. Agents' drove around the ice cream truck, bribing some with free ice cream for any information on the inside of Dr. Delbert's home. Not knowing anything about the kid's secret pact, but all were still given free ice cream that day. Few of them found kids who wanted to earn a few dollars jumping at the chance to become better citizens. One evening, new kids approached Dr. Gilbert back yard to play with his kids who were not allowed to come due to harassment.

Back down on Planet Nimble, Ruler Zubbler concluded that there was no need to pull the fake planet virus's stunt in order to force vax these aliens, because their first plans were working perfectly. The sky watchers and his forces have even the militants' ones under control, but they never guess the real warriors from above earth about to strike them.

On a warm cloudy weekend, Professor Dilbert, Monk Train, Superman, Madam Butterfly, and Spiderman stood deep in the huge forest in the tenth-dimensional matrix. The shadow regime forces never knew they were there about to go fight an interspace battle above them. The two bright suns set in the west and south, the five gazing down at Neo. He closed his eyes for a second, with a smile on his face expecting a big surprise of any kind. "Neo walked closer up to them, saying step toward let us hold hands, my friends. "Now, Look, Madam Butterfly do not transform until the day of the battle, you all must look like ordinary earth tourists." "Oh, I like being a tourist she happily said." "Good for you Madam, now Superman hid your Cape/x-x-ray glasses, Spiderman no climbing outside buildings, Monk no shift changing or jazz music playing from your shoulders weaponries, so now, got all that out of the way. "Just one more thing, Professor play down your intellects, no what I mean sir." "Sure, do Neo, in other words, play dumb oh yes got it he said." "Madam Butterfly glances over at all Monk Train, Superman, thinking I had both of them, got to work on the Professor next get some of his energy, and smile. The warriors forming a ring around the tree as a heavy gravity force engulfed them. All the space satellites and computers devices became useless for the next thirty minutes, not able to penetrate their dimension. Even the ground agents that watches the forest for terrorist groups had no clue at that moment an interspace war was about to take place right under their noses. Neo forest friends watches from a distance, knowing what is about to go down. As they stood there, gazing at the huge forest trees Neo turned invisible, flew swiftly around each one quickly, and touched them with a powerful jolt. A tingling sensation started at their feet has worked its way up through their bodies. All their eyes became shut tight, ears stopped up and bodies became paralyze, that instant yellowish-orange bright color energy brighter than the suns enter their bodies. Neo spoke to them briefly from the inside of their eardrums, stating three direct comments. "You all have different skills sets, will work as a team becoming one main energy source and we will defeat them." The huge trees were suddenly engulfed with heavy gray fogs as Monk Train them paralyzed bodies floated inside the mist; they all were still conscious.

The gateway open, they lifted up slowly and glided down silent on a journey through the portal threshold. No one had any fear at that moment, noises were coming from a distance drumming sounds that vibrated the air around them with little effect on their bodies. Their bodies whirl around and around like little mini dancing tornados in slow motion. Their physiques begin to stretch and bounce similar to rubber bands. Neo is still invisible in the center, using his energy force as a transported vehicle. From him came a bright shining light putting fleeing shadows on the tunnel interior walls. Once spilled into this new world grounds like little ants, they floated around for a few minutes drinking in the beautiful colorful sites. Dr Gilbert rubbing his arms to see if it was still attached. "This is really cool, do feel a little lightheaded, but I'm ok he said with a smile." They all have shrined down to the size of the three feet tall Nimble Aliens to align with their environment. Using Isotopes flares around the portal exit way from earth, half of Neo's energy was lost at that moment. "Listen up, Neo said, you all would be gone for one hour, which will equal to four hours on the earth time cycle. Safely you all will return to the surfaces.

"Alarms went off, security announces over the communication systems unarmed earth aliens have entered Planet Nimble's territory." Neo quickly bid them farewell quickly, exit back up the portal toward earth, fear of capture not wanting to be discovered as not being a clone. Sky-Watcher flew over them observing with weapons drawn. Their Commander warns them over the radio, "Report, do not detain them and send me streaming video images of every move they make."

The Professor now felt since Neo split the scene, they were at risk of being harmed. "No, my friend, I will take it from here, Monk told them." They observed the aliens looking like giants compared to the shrinks to their bodies to fit into this world. Be careful, where you walk said a voice that sounded like his friend, Neo," "See, you need to change your mind, return said the Professor." We will say I never left smile Neo, but he was just a clone." "I know who you all are, Madam Butterfly, Jazz Man Monk train, Superman and Spiderman oh yes, different skills set this going be good said Neo."

Suddenly five little Nimble girls approached them asking in a strange language where are you from?" As their three heads on each body stares at them smiling. "Some heads came up close whispering in their ears; I know how to speak some of your language." "You talk to them Neo because we do not know how to communicate back to them said the Professor..." "Ok said Neo, I told them you all are my friends  What else did you say, he asked again?" I told them you are from planet earth on the top surfaces outside of Nimble Star world." "When can they come to our world, see how we lived Neo, Dr.

Delbert asked?" "Your world might not accept them being very different from humans at this moment. See, you have certain groups of humans that have primitive problems with the skin colors of a person and have built a false narrative around such foolishness. Any intelligent aliens would not want to get in contact or be around such sick-minded groups under any conditions. So, in order to visit earth all of them and us down here, we have to become invisible aliens, go into a fifth dimension or higher just for Peace's sake. They spend trillions of dollars flying up in space settling there to find intelligent life, every alien knows their way of thinking. We have been amongst humans since the beginning of our evolution watching and listening to everything earth does. However, those highly advanced alien races cannot interfere, unless given orders to stop the madness on earth; quite sure Monk knows what I mean. "Yep, it's called karma, the big payback, I know about universal justice, its laws, which is an equalizer Monk said." "Me, I blend in as an ordinary old short man on earth Neo said, which is the way everybody on earth sees me. With Nimble, it is completely different.

Nevertheless, you all standing before me now knows my identity and this place now. Dr. Delbert looked over toward the Nimble Star girls. "Neo said; we must go, the little girls' heads smile and said goodbye in echoing sound voices."

Superman went over to look at some rocks that gave off strange sounds. The rocks were spending around them, giving off rays of different lights and colors. "Take us with you, they begged." "No, we cannot do that, said Superman." "Somehow two of the smallest one landed in his shirt pocket without him knowing it. "Let's all go over to this university that sets in the sky, Neo said." "We all down for that Madam Butterfly loudly chanted with delight. "Speaking of that, look we are walking on air." But it feels like solid ground, said Spiderman." "Everybody just follows me Neo stated" "Wish we could do this back home and not ride in silly cars, Dr. Delbert excitedly blurted out., but you guys can, he told his four friends" High up in the sky they saw all type of Nimble Star citizens flying without wings and Solar Pirates watching them. The closer they came toward the university, a few seconds later, the building shape's structure, and color gradually changed. "Next the buildings begin verbally talking to us, "see we have visitors from a faraway land, welcome here at Nimble Knowledge Center, and enjoy the stay." Everybody began to laugh, pointing at the talking buildings, not believing what was taking place before them.

As they came up to a closed door, they disappear right through it directly into a classroom. The top star students teaching each other verbally, without books or computers capable of retaining all knowledge. Future experiences gains as they grew into adults and learned from their wise elders. "I wish our universities could let us teach each other like this and get rid of books, uttered Dr. Delbert." "That would be fun, but they have something you all do not have. See you comparing your world to ours; we do not need books and computers to get information's Neo stated." So, you are trying to say we depend on technology, they use brains, so that makes them smarter." "Now, you are saying there is no right or wrong here, just different folks." "What I'm going to do Dr. Delbert… let you all teach each other about your different worlds Neo said." "That will be fun, who do you think we should ask about doing this?" "Maybe, we should ask that person over there peeking at us, giggled Monk."

At that very moment, a Solar Pirate Professor came over and said, we cannot have strangers talking to our students, move along." One of the rocks flew out of Superman's shirt pocket and travel toward the Pirate. "Instant she turns around exclaiming, you all are welcome to set in on this class just for today." Dr. Delbert looked at his warrior friends and Neo not believing what had just occurred. Professor thinking since I reconsider, recording what they say about earth lives would help benefit our future invasion.

Next couple of hours, they learned about Nimble Star world. "They are just like the Solar Pirates around here filled with fear, wants to rule and control groups they think that they are less intelligent, stated a student."

Eventually, barriers will be open for your world and mines he whispers to the students." The dense forest brought people from around the world to our doorsteps another student stated; it's a gateway to us." "That is very unusual to have one special area on earth and opens up a door to a different world, stated Madam Butterfly."

Neo whispers to Dr Dilbert, we all know the Solar Pirates are losing their grip to control us, they know the words out all-over Nimble Star. We are gradually getting our light energy back, soon we will be able to time travel like everyone else's. "I heard that, Superman said, as he kept pushing the rocks back in his pocket." Now, he knows their value and what they are capable of doing in a tight situation, thank God it is not kryptonite to make me weak.

"Tell you what; I will meet the Solar Pirate Leader Ruler Zubbler later, now since they do not have much of a choice to stop progress. They might grant certain ones from earth temporary stay to learn our Languages. That would be a good idea stated Monk, do you think they pick me?" Depends mostly on how you make them feels about you, here in Nimble, we can speak over two hundred languages." How is that possible, when only we speak many languages where we come from. Maybe growing up, you had no interest in learning a new culture. "But before we meet the Solar Pirate Leaders, I will teach you a few of my native tongue, it's never too late to learn anything..."

The Professor waved goodbye to all the students and Professors as they floated from the University. Distance away Sky Watchers troops spied and trail them above the floating buildings that acts as a shield of protection. Let us all go over toward that in that direction uttered Neo. Yes, that is a good idea said Spiderman, above them, floated a large mountain of rocks and trees in midair. "Neo, how do we walk through this forest, Professor asked?" "Same way you do back home just walk, but don't look down, he said." For the next hour, they traveled on foot. "Why are we walking instead of flying Monk asked?" We are not allowed to fly through the forest on this planet, unless on the basis of extreme emergency he said. Slowly making their way without hearing anything, all of a certain loud noise's rushes toward them.

"Ten large Nimble Star Sky-Watcher men landed near the forest with lots of different faces on each body, Solar Pirates rulers by their side." In a loud voice, all said at the same time, we sense humans amongst us. "This is a violation of our Forest Old World Order, take them away now." The Sky Watchers obeyed the voice of the Pirate Commander, placing an electronic chained cuff on their necks. Instantly, they all lost the rest of his powers. Neo turned; looked at Monk, with a real sad eye, not like the big strong aggressive alien back on earth. "No, you cannot take us away, they all screamed at the alien creatures," Superman whispers telling his rocks to take action. "No, no, we must not let them see us they said, you are all on your own now." "Do not try to stop them, remember if they ask a question, just keep quiet, Neo sadly told them." I wander where we are going, Professor thought. "Nobody can save you, little earth folks, so come along one giant Sky-Watcher commanded." Now, they were able to understand a little bit of the Language he was speaking because of the university they stop.

Without answering, they grab and place all of us inside a shiny golden-looking birdcage. Locked inside, the cage grew colorful wings and flew alongside the Sky Watchers singing songs. They flew over strange buildings that spoke to us just like the school and their appearance looked like trees cities skyscrapers. "Where are you taking us to, they all screamed out again." Neo told us not to say anything, Monk reminded the professor." The giant creatures never entertain their questions, landed at a large building made out of a cluster of trees and glass.

Enter the building without going through a door again. On the other side, thousands of Nimble Star Sky Watchers looking just like the ones that brought us here. The light energy coming from their bodies was artificial brilliant light, so they can be controlled by Solar Pirates Leaders. My wife and kids, I should have told them the truth about Neo, Dr. Delbert, thought again. Now, I got all my earth friends trapped in this mess with me. Monk Train and Superman why are you all not using your superpowers on their butts. In due time Professor; Monk told him, you got to see what I'm working with." "That's right Madam Butterfly said and looked over at Monk, he winks at her." Oh yes, yes, his clone recognizes me she thought.

They walked across a huge indoor bridge as they looked down into a large room saw abducted humans from the outer world top surfaces. "Next, a fat Solar Pirate lady with many a single small head stated, what trouble brings them all here, she asked a sky watcher?" The rest of her heads started looking them up and down. "Violating rules of many things in the forest your majesty, along with a friend from here, he said." "Where is that Neo, I know it's him trying to be friendly to everybody above us she said, I do not care for humans." "We detained Neo back over in a cell placing him with all the other traitors who brought the humans trash into our new sacred world." "Many times, I have warned those gatekeepers, might have to retire him from dimensional traveling to other worlds, she stated." "These little humans' tourists have no permission from the Solar Leaders committee to be her boss, he stated." "Ok, send them over to the humans holding cell block, when their cases come up, let them determined their fate, should make them work without pay in the sun factory." "Get these filthy-looking humans' creatures out of my sight she screams to the Sky Watchers." "A group of huge guards stood behind as they followed the lead Watcher to this large area, this will be your home, so get in one of them shouted at us."

Standing there observing hundreds of captured earth peoples sleeping and some chatting to each other. "An elderly lady came over; I see some high and mighty alien got you all up in here too." "Honey, there are some mean suckers up in here, they told me I will see the Solar Pirate Leader a year ago." "Monk stares at the lady, how long have you been here miss, he asked?" "Going to two years, I should have never kept that alien secret, yes never should I have she kept repeating." "What alien are you talking about, was his name Neo, Dr. Delbert asked?" "His name was Golden Star, she answered." "Know what I think, they send different ones with these magical abilities to the surfaces to lure us dumb ones into their traps." "Since I have been in here, just about all the stories are the same, except for three hundred, talking aliens looking like birds lured them in here."

Madam Butterfly, smiling, remembering the dense forest in Utah, probably the same birds I saw, wander why they never talk to me." So, really, the gatekeeper for this world lures peoples in a trap, the old woman said. "Honey, he uses his wits and charms to weasel you all here, so that must be their entire motive, she said." "They got lots of us in the sweat suns making factories making dam suns so they keep and sells them to other planets down here." "So, they are using any humans they capture as slaves to do some of their dirty jobs, Professor asked her." Yes, without pay, guess we cannot spend their kink of money, they don't have any... another man said."

"The old lady said it all got started when we came on a tour bus to Utah Mountains for a three-week vacation." "You know a bunch of old folks, this strange little old man started following me acting very friendly." "Everybody started teasing me about I found a man. Next thing that crazy man actually started talking to me more, then I end up here like a fool one night, he's nowhere in sight now. "Now, can you believe that's all this fairytale bull going on around here?" "I believe you mama; because certain men take advantage and seduce us women, but sometimes, we join in just to enjoy the pleasures, Madam Butterfly said." I admit you are right old lady like me gets horny sometimes, so when the right guy comes along pushes my buttons things happen, she said with a laugh." "Know something else woman now he rocked my world and had me begging for more she said." "Look mama, I think I have heard enough wild stories for tonight, Madam Butterfly said and walks back over toward her warrior friends."

The rest of the earth people suddenly started feeling sleepy and went to lay on their large floor pillows. For the next hour or so, the old woman talking over there to anyone that had the patience to listen. Dr. Delbert fell asleep. Monk clone, Superman, Spiderman stayed awoke to keep an eye on the crew and the others, not trusting this strange place. Superman looking down at Madam Butterfly sleeping decided to place a blanket over her to stay warm. "No, no she said, I rather take my chances without that on me, no telling what in those blankets." The lights over the area soon got dimmer and low jazz music you can sleep by started playing. She gets up walks away saying, do not trust this place, looking around in the semidarkness for Dr. Delbert as he laid down and got under his blanket. "What are you thinking about, wifely, now while we are in this stressful place, I can be here for you... you know what I mean." She reaches down and squeezes him, he reaches and felt her up until she almost screams out in ecstasy. Monk Train looks over toward them thinking, there she goes again, and we at war, but who am I to judge. Superman slips his gasses on using his x-ray vision, saw through the blanket what they were doing, thinking I figured she was not ready to settle down, but whom I am to find a fault or judge. "Not here Dr Delbert said, too many people around, we make too much noise." A guy heard Madam Butterfly moaning near him, not here he whispers, go ask that guard over there under that dim light at a desk for a bedroom in the back for your privacy."

"Ok, she whispers to him, pulling her skirt down pushing back the blanket cover she strolled over talks and laugh briefly with the guard. Now, they are both inside a small private single bed helping each other undress. "The Professor looks at her, you are good at getting what you want from them; maybe you can stop this hot war about to come off." "Baby, right now, the only thing coming off is my black panties, you and me getting off, you know what I mean, thinking I'm not going to let him know I'm a shapeshifter." "She said in a sexy tone baby lift me off the bed and walk around I'll be holding onto you tightly." "Both feet planted on the floor Professor stood wide-legged over the single bed, as she laid nude on the sheets. Next, he reaches down while standing and place both hands under her a** lifted her up off the bed, she wrapping her long legs around his waist. With one hand gripping the headboard, and the other one holding her a**, she held on tightly in midair. There, she was high in the air calling the Professor's name repeatedly, this was a completely new position she ever had loving every minute of it. This gave her total freedom to wiggle upon him hard, driving him out of his mind. He got so excited moved away from the bed walking slowly around the room with me grinding the hell out of him. I held on tightly my arms around his neck, now he had both hands gripping my wet romp, dam soon he exploded letting out a loud moan. He eases me back down onto the soft bed, kissing me for few minutes then he mounted on me. A few hours later that night, he gave her what she wanted, Madam Butterfly more than pleased when Professor gave her his private number to be able to call once they return up to earth. With a smile, at least, he lives here in Utah and I can see him whenever I am pleased. I have all that out of the way ready to kick some butts now. She and the Professor sneaked back out onto the floor cover up pretended they were asleep.

The next morning, bright lights coming from the Sky watcher's energy gave off a slight pulsating warmest. The sun we see that rises like true clockwork every morning from the east back on earth was nowhere on this unusual planet. From their bodies, lights came, which in turn, illuminates the entire environment, higher their conscious, more light given off. All the Sky Watchers creatures were controlled by signal frequencies codes built into their artificial lights. Even outside, it is bright from the Nimble people, shadows castes in countless directions. Now, whenever Solar Pirates shows up in a large group, a huge floating sun star controller satellite will appear in the sky, until they leave. Their bodies feed off this high artificial energy and weaken all the creatures so they would not be attacked by them. Monk saw this as a weakness after studying how they move around on the planet that is the reason they took all the light energy from aliens. To create this floating mega sun just to sustain their life on this planet, without it, they will become weaker and soon perish.  With the help of earth friends to bring the lights back into his people, they can destroy this artificial sun. However, Monk being without his dimensional powers to go secretly into their hidden bases to check them. Ruler Zubbler has clones of these suns, knowing in advance that if a strike takes out that one, automatic replacement takes place. Monk knows they need to locate the entire areas they are kept in order to destroy them,

Dr. Delbert realizing Neo is a true friend to save all of them from being missing back home. When his friends came to visit him in solitary confinement that night, he sends them a mental thought of what to do without uttering a word. The time they travel back into their world as clones pretending to be there, still living amongst them. Their loved ones back home never knew the difference. Even in the classroom, students and professors had no clue that Dr. Delbert was a clone. "Sometimes, his wife will say things like, you are acting like your head stuck in the clouds come back to earth to him." Nevertheless, the clones have been created not to have too much humans' emotions, pretended not to hear those foolish things coming from them.

Talking direct to relatives about loved ones being missing, they have known idea what happen to them. We think some of them are alive, but in another place, we cannot get to them. Some relatives and loved ones never saying a word to the press, decided to go up in the area and look themselves. Digging around trees, checking caves, under brushes not knowing their loved ones are being held hostage by aliens' right below their feet.

Rewards of missing peoples on the local and international news broadcast weekly; all have traveled to the forest in Utah. The agents never gave any hint beings from another world might be the cause, the state is now nicknamed Utah Triangle. Now, the secret regime agents knew they have a good case, to remove everybody off the forest trails again. Declaring the area had a mutated virus strain that could not be cured; this would frighten all the joggers to stay out of the area. If you are caught in the areas jogging, you will be house arrested, vaccinated with a chip for tracking within twenty-four hours. Signs placed all up down the trails, which kept most out.

The noisy neighbor decided to tell the agents he followed Dr. Delbert around once a week. This is to get back at him for reporting him to the neighborhood association for a yard violation fine.  Snitching on Dr. Delbert and his friends gave him pleasure and big paydays, hoping this will help to bring peace to the small neighborhood. Telling them, he overheard the group talking about another world in the forest, but could not get its name. From that day forward, they paid visits to that neighbor's house just about every day asking him tons of questions. Building a stronger profile and case on putting Dr. Delbert in the hot seat. Everywhere Doc's family went, the agents followed close by. His wife never told a soul once he gave her a fake story about things that happen at the university; she meditated hoping that everything will just go away. Now, Dr. Delbert is caught up between two webs. His real body down on planet Nimble, here he was on earth living as a clone, not even the agents or wife had no clue.

Back in Nimble Star world, detained now for a month, without seeing the Solar Pirate leader. Madam Butterfly and the old woman became close friends, who reminds her of an aunt. Everybody else sets along worrying about how to get back home up to earth. They are not confined to a closed-cell with bars, free to walk around and socialize with the other captured humans. My name is Rosette, what are you all names, the lady asked?' "My name is Madam Butterfly, they over there are all my friends she stated." Your friend Monk very popular Jazz musician has lots of followers she said to her." That does not matter now Ms. Rosette, we all must find a way to get back home she whispers. "You all, it does not make any difference to me, back home, I was on a trip for elders, said, Rosette." They told me not to trust that strange-looking man talking to me at that time, but he became my lover and my best friend. "Yes, yes, you told me that story when we first got down here, she said." "I guess back there in that small mountain town they have probably gotten tired of searching for me, as she drops her head." Dr. Delbert then not realizing, in a few more hours an attempted coup will occur to try and rescue them all.

That moment thousands of five-headed aliens down on the main streets below shouting freedom and release all prisons now. Chanting echoing sounds of Solar Pirates will lose all their artificial sunlight energy soon and will not be able to control us, Nimble Star citizens, anymore. All the talking buildings were putting this newsbreak out on the streets. "That's talking about you all, must be someone special to them, said another lady." Some of the protester's heads began to pop in and out of the walls chanting different names of prisoners, freedom is near do you hear. Every capture human's eye turned toward their group. One man said, I see you all are the answers to everybody getting out of here, thank you very much. They smiled and waved at Dr. Delbert, Rosetta whispers to them when they come to take you all into the room to ask a million questions, you do not have to say anything to them. The Sky Watchers started arresting the protesters that came through the walls. More they arrested that day; replacements came quickly to the streets.

The Solar Pirate woman that wrote them up came and summon all to the office. "Seems like your little five-team crew have corrupted the rest of the prisoners, I do not like that." You all have been causing great problems since you have been here, so the Solar Pirates Leaders are personal coming to pick all of you up."   A Nimble sky Watcher commander stated to them, "you all influencing the peoples outside these walls to think life is better beyond here." "Even though, I am a born and raise Nimble Star by birthright; I want things to stay the way they are." "We are all comfortable and like our jobs working for the Solar Pirates, cannot see ourselves doing anything else." "I am personally going to take you all in the backroom, erase your memory before they get here." They will see how dumb and stupid you all are in comparing you with us. "I want the ring leader which is Dr. Delbert go down on the street. Listen carefully, tell those losers you all are ok and love it here, do I make myself clear?" "Not saying a word, he just gave the commander a mean look, like I do not care what you do." Suddenly, a chubby Pirate woman enters the room and started yelling; "you five fools are in big trouble now as her pierce voice echo throughout the room." She was trying to confuse them as they all played dumb and poked their tongue out at her. "Sky-Watcher took them both into the brains recycle room; since you won't obey our order to go down there. Now, you all would regret ever coming here to our world she snapped."

"Let's go fool, so we can get this over with, shouted Monk," as they wage a war of the mind on their captors. Once in the dark cold room, seeing millions of floating heads of different colors. Some rub upon them, not saying a word for the next few hours, they let their minds go blank. Their way of emotions about the Sky-Watcher was captured as a digital image footprint. A few seconds later, it was uploaded into mechanical robot brains that looks like each one of them. Soon all fifty robots appears before them. The warriors' stares at each one without blinking an eye, unbelievable they could do such a thing, Dr Delbert thought. "His look-alike robot sounding just like him, asked him, do you like it here?" Not answering anything this fake piece of crap asked him, this fool using reverse psychology. At the end of question five hundred, the robots disappear from sight without saying another word. Next was loud echoing rap music, Superman then decided to dance. "We know you are lurking in here somewhere lady, got any more tricks up your sleeves old bat, Spiderman yelled out?" By now, they knew what they were up to, gave them exactly that, not thinking about anything for the next thirty minutes.

Soon the guards came, brought them back upstairs, these earth creeps minds are free, let the dumbest get their belongings and board the Solar Pirates Ships Sky Watchers, she commanded."

The Solar Pirates Leader Ruler Zubbler floated around Dr. Delbert and his crew glaring at them without saying anything. They both stood together standing in a circular group, staring back at the enemy without fear. Now, they did not like that, wanting them to be afraid and asking to be spared of any kind of harsh punishments. For the next ten minutes, this stare-down went on, until one of the Pirate guards broke his silence. "Look, you, earth creatures… let's cut through the chase, we are still in control here, and there's nothing you can do about it. "Even if you try, you cannot win this battle." "The Nimble peoples all loves and want us here, it is you outsiders coming in and trying to give them brighter ideas." "What the buildings announced about us losing control is nonsense, they have been programmed with the wrong information." "So, who is the spokesperson, speak up quickly he commanded?"

"Without hesitation, Monk clone stepped forward, look fatso, we know what time it is, you are playing that this world is crumbling as I stand before you." "So, Lady Majestic gave us false information about how unlearned you all were, but I see you speak with intelligent." "But that's beside the point, why are you all here meddling in our great society businesses?" "We invited ourselves after we heard the cries of them wanting to be free." The winds of time blowing through the leaves on a huge forest came from these poor Nimble Star peoples, he told him.

Ruler Zubbler and his guards floated around the warrior without uttering a word quickly disappear in midair for a second and came right back in view. "Look, we have forest trees everywhere that gives out phony cries for help and we treat them back to being their healthy selves. "Look, a man like our leader said, your world is falling and the Nimble Star peoples you captured know it, shouted Madam Butterfly." Five guards rush over toward her, take your hands off me, she screamed at them." Monk laughs, realizing she must pull it together. Ruler Zubbler floated around them to try to find who was not intelligent. Both of them seem to be smart, wise, and not except a bribe to turn on each other. Dr Delbert never said a word; he felt Monk was doing a good job telling those fat clowns off.

Monk, Superman, Spiderman made a dash for the floating satellite sun above Ruler Zubbler and his crew. They threw off their regular tourist clothing revealing the real warriors increasing in sizes, they grab at the sun smashing it to the ground. "Guards capture those four clowns bring them so I can take pleasure in destroying them myself yelled Ruler Zubbler." That very moment the energy around the enemy faded from them and the sky watchers fell from the sky as they went dim.

Go to the forest, go grab another sun yelled Zubbler almost out of breath as a group of sky watchers dashes to the sun factory hidden in the floating forest. Monk remembers what Neo said, you can only fly in the forest on a special occasion, dam, if this is not special. They followed the running Sky Watchers, Monk decided to transform himself into a Planet Nimble spaceship and place himself in their pathway. Once they came closer, they told the pilots this is an emergency and that they must take control and they flew away thousands of miles away into the dark thick floating forest. Superman used the voice guidance computer to fly and locate the factory as Monk listen in to get them there quicker. Once all the input were downloaded for sun factory, he instantly reprogrammed the ship back to Ruler Zubbler location. Monk them detached themselves from the transformed spaceship and went on over to the sun factory. This is too good he yelled out; they are going to be disappointed in a few minutes. As he enters the factory seeing all the Planet Nimbler dimly lit faces and earth slaves' workers on assembler lines sweating pouring off their faces. He got on the intercom "this emergency, all works leave their work station and go outside now." Monk used his saxophone and broadcasts over the planet, even to buildings making an announcement; "CITIZENS OF NIMBLE WITH ORIGINAL LIGHTS FORM A LINK, HOLD HANDS WHERE EVER YOU ARE AND GET IN CIRCLE GROUPS NOW." "OK ALL EARTH CITIZENS WORKERS STAND BACK OVER HERE and THANK YOU." Superman went around to all buildings using his x-ray visons peering through the layers seeing more Pirates supervisors hiding. Spiderman leaps from each buildings using his webs, wrapping them up with his sticky webs like ropes. Madam Butterfly came along scooped them up placing them into a holding cell electronic force field.

The Solar Pirates were confused now, trying to figure out what went wrong. Do not just stand their guards get at them he shouted; the Sky Watchers Guards refuse to obey their commands." A little bit too late, all the Nimble's 'rush toward the sky with a special shield of protection, rays from the enemy's weapons bounce off their bodies. From the floating forest area Superman, channel down earth sun energy through the portal entranceway. Most of the Solar Pirates knocked off their feet due to the great power surges, bouncing around like basketballs, losing total control. The sun energy charges were dispersed to the Nimble's bodies through the planet. Pirates' overseers told the loyal Sky Watchers to capture all the warrior forces, as they fired their weapons, the rest of them attempted to get a sun back up. All their artificial sun kept going dim, it needed direct contact with the worker's energies, and none was insight to fuel it, this causes a chain reaction to all the Pirates. Their artificial lights left their bodies and went into the last sun suddenly it exploded in midair, and then, fell out of the Nimble Planet sky. Once on the ground, its solar energy seeped into the soil crying and weeping to send an urgent signal for another clone sun to replace it. Madam Butterfly, Monk Train, Superman, Spiderman, and Nimble Sky Watchers Guards reached deep into the enemy headquarter and bombard the entire clone's suns factories. Cheers went up from outside workers who now have new natural lights replacement reattached. The Sky Watchers realizing that they are completely returned to their normal behavior finish rounding up all the Solar Pirates and their guard's drones. Ruler Zubbler and his guards escaped into a hidden ship and left Nimble Planet. Superman x-ray vision spotted them inside the ship, Spiderman spewed out lots of webs to prevent a takeoff and Monk came aboard to tell the Chief time up, his guard fired lasers beams bullets. Suddenly, Madam Butterfly decided not to transform completely into a butterfly, kept her earthly figure with wings attached to her shoulders. "Monk did a double-take, this is war baby, he hurriedly places a shield... between them came snatched Ruler Zubbler away from his guards in another dimension. Madam Butterfly flew into the dimension with them using her power to spin a sticky solution around him.

The guards looks around like a bunch of fools, not able to see them, hell what the sense to continue fighting for the boss one said." That's right, stated Spiderman lay all weaponries down now." "Hell, who this freak, hanging upside down dress in that weird clown outfit think he's talking to them all started laughing." Ok, been warned fools, as they tried to pick up their weapon, a web was shot and snatch from his hands." If we all reach down on the counts of three this fool cannot zap all at one time, at least one of us put his lights out." "Ok, try me, Spiderman said with a laugh, as a matter of fact, I'll count, one, two. Three." As they reach, he zaps all the guns at them, blew on his two fingers now, what you have to say. "All standing there looking stunned, raised their hands up and surrendered an electronic force field place around them. Spiderman, Superman went into the seventh dimension where Monk was. Ok, we go the main character of this revolt Superman said; maybe, we should turn him over to the Nimble citizens." "Now, man you know that's the best ideas I've heard since I have been here, yea see how they handle his fat tale laugh Monk," I agree said Spiderman, this can be the end for him, a new beginning for Nimble Aliens." Ruler Zubbler head down, not wanting to face the citizens, look, let me go back where I came from there won't be any more problems from me." "Now, do you think we are foolish enough to stand here and believe this bull sh*t, do any of you guys believe Monk asked?" Hell, no said Superman, but I must point out good try

Chief." I sure do not believe him, this con man will go and bring back reinforcement tyrants like him, he never gives up, Spiderman states, let's see what the Nimble's say."

Back over at Planet Nimble, the real Neo flew up toward the sky his clones met and reenter his body. Dr. Delbert and the entire captured earth group free from prison looked up from the ground because of all the bright lights moving around in the sky. This made them see the illusion of this world from a totally new perspective. As they stood, Neo proudly looked at the earth folks; vowing never to let this happen again. You all have helped to restore our world back to the way it once was. The Leader of Nimble Star came forth announced all citizens were free after the Solar Pirate defeat.

The huge Sky-Watcher's stood listening to their leader that day, decided not to let any Pirates out. "The Solar pirates not knowing what punishment lies ahead for them, since their leader dumped them, perhaps they bribe their way out of this. Let us put the enemies on trial a few citizens yelled out, that's right shouted the old lady Rosette."

Lo and behold in a matter of minutes someone yelled that Pirates hiding out in the building basement with hostages. Special Sky Watchers agents arrive on the scene gradually they scan the whole place observing for a second, went in to free the hostages.

Seconds later, Dr. Delbert recognized a familiar group of faces as special agents from the earth that trailed him each day. They paid no mind to anyone standing there, just glancing around at the buildings, because they were in this world through a dream. Sky Watchers shouted at them to leave or be arrested. "No, said the Nimble leader, those are Dr. Delbert's friends from the earth, no harm shall come to them." A few Watchers Guards still felt the urge to kick butt disobeying orders, started battling the earth agents using no weapons, just hands to hands combat style. One agent gave a good kick with his head to one of the Sky Watchers.

"Dr. Delbert, I know you saw all your earth friends back there, they were not real. "All of them at home right now have the same dreams about rescuing everybody. But once they awaken, they will not remember any of it." "Dr.

Delbert thought, but I still have lots of explaining about them not being my friend, but my enemies back on earth. "Do not worry you been covered; the agents would never be able to transport here… Neo told him and winked his eye."

As Neo stood looking over the warrior and the Nimble Leaders. "A little voice said what about me, who has to get back where I never trust another little old man again, Rosette, uttered." "No, if I give you some of my dimensional powers mama this will never happen in my world again, you could fight off the evil ones." "I do not need any of your dumb stupid powers Neo, she told him." "He just smiled at her; maybe Monk Train can give you powers to protect yourself in the future when you return to my world." "Like I said dummy, never want to come back here she stated again, everybody laughs." Oh yes, I will be glad to have that protection myself from those mean fat monsters with all those small heads, Professor said." All captured human beings are free to go back home, the leaders announced."

Soon, the four warriors appears back with Ruler Zubbler arrested in a golden cage with flying wings attached. "A cheer went up from the crowd, at last, they said, let us deal with him, yes put his fat tail on trial yelled Rosetta." "That lady has the right talking point Superman told Monk Train." "Hell yes, Monk said, Ok folks listen up, we are going to let you all determine his fate earth warriors to turn the Ruler Zubbler over to your Court System."

A hedge of protection was placed around the entrance into Nimble Star, earth satellites would not be able to map or transmit any signal from this location. With all energy, back the Nimble aliens travel to other dimensions beyond earth, and soon leaves on the forest trees are never used again for escaping. Shadow regime agents kept working around the clock, looking for a breakthrough; never once seeing Delbert enter his home that night. However, they heard talk from Dr. Delbert's nosey neighbor about this underground hidden world without any proof. They had their engineers send down sonar rockets to x-ray the areas, but Space Constar Umar place a blockage layer to give false readings to their computers. Soon they pull back tried their satellites to map deeper areas around the planet for any indication of a hidden world, all images came back negative.

Once back home, the professor went upstairs finding his lovely Cindy and his clone making out, she was screaming and moaning. He stood there feeling jealousy watching her legs wrapped around this clone begging him not to stop. Standing there for two hours, never want me no more than fifteen minutes. Maybe, I should only see Madam Butterfly she is very excited we go for hours. "She asked the clone, baby, what got into you lately, bring back the young girl I once was doing it like this pushing all the right buttons. After hearing her tell him all that maybe I should just leave them two together seem like she is happier. The clone never said a word rather he keeps making love to her. I had enough of listening and watching him spoil her, went in the room taps him on the shoulders. He looks up at me and instantly disappears, I enter my wife she never knew afterward we fell asleep in each other arms.

"That morning, she reaches over kisses me, good morning, Mr. Stud she said, what's gotten into you lately honey but its ok with me." "Well, baby you know stress can make some people's sex drive stronger, with all these agents harassing us," That morning, he got up shower and dressed for work, walks out of the door looking at all the jeeps park on his street they all watching him and neighbors.

"Driving to work, he laughs they going to all that trouble the war over down on Planet Nimble's." But I wander she expects me to perform like that every week. Have to find a way to keep my clone around for emergency use. I guess the kids must not have noticed I was living as a clone amongst them, the two dogs knew but just kept it a secret. As he turned the corner two men glances at him in a strange kind of way, maybe they know. As usual, a van followed at a distance behind his car. Once on campus, all his students treated him as if he was never missing.

After returning from work that day, maybe this time I will go and stay much longer in Neo's world, he thought. That evening, touching the door, and went straight through it. Excited, walking toward the huge dense forest vanishes right into their world. Neo has given me these limited powers to do this on my own, without him being here. He stood there near a floating tree and came back straight into the room in an instant. "Tiger, the dog on stacks of books stares at him, I will take you with me the next time I go, Delbert told him." settling back at the desk to do write a more rough draft about his real-life adventure on Nimble. Later, went downstairs to watch the seven-o'clock news with his family. "Dad, you sure been acting strange lately, his son stated, you do not let us go with you to jog anymore, why." "You kids cut down on the noise, he has to deal with lots of students every day needs to relax, his wife stated." As they watched a story about an elder woman named Rosetta returning home after being rescued by a dog. Holloway Star studios wants to do a movie about her ordeal, because she has told them some weird out-of-this-world stories. Hearing this, Dr. Delbert, came closer to the TV thinking that's my friend from Nimble Star. Dad, you are getting too close up on the TV, cannot see through you, Alice stated." "Johnny snicker, while are you so interest in that old bat story, just an average news story dad, bet she did not like it there at the old folk's home and left."

Now, she is talking out of her head about aliens, such nonsense I have not seen any around here his wife joking stated." As he continues watching the TV Delbert thinking if only you all knew the truth, he all most burbled out those words. How they were able to make a news story that quickly about her. When the old man appeared on the news without revealing his identity, but it was Neo. "There goes dad's friend, old man Charlie that's walks on the forest trail, his son yelled out laughing." Dr. Delbert eased back up to his room; Neo must have taken the old woman back home he thought.

He locked the door, stood in the center of the room. With eyes closed and called Neo's name in his mind." Eventually, he picked up his brain waves signal just like an iPhone connection. "That moment he answers him, I'm all right Dr. Delbert, out here in California." "Yes, I know, seen you and Rosette have made the national news and now talking about making a movie together." "How could you do that as a friend Neo, he asked him?"" Maybe that's why you dumped your powers on me, to not be bothered again." "No, Dr. Delbert, you are wrong, I have to do certain things in humans' understanding." "All the others capture earth humans were let go by Nimble Leaders, their memories have been erased about being there. "The agents interviewed Rosetta here, but she was not able to give them any real information about Nimble, I block some memories from her. "Now, they think she just got a strong imagination and just want attention." "Your mind was not totally erased by this epic event, because of you being a thinker." "Monk, Superman, Madam Butterfly, and Spiderman are the only mortal ones that can keep secrets, that's why they are given powers by the Space Aliens Federation Constar Umar."

Constar, he contacted Monk at home lying down on the sofa; my friend thinks for saving Planet Nimble. I am keeping my words you must have powers to go through many tough challenges back here on Nimble, I know your music concert be coming up soon weeks away down there. "Nimble's as a friend has the will and courage to obtain a life not living under fear." "Constar you seem to have full confidence in Nimble's Monk said." Tell you what Monk Train; I will let all four of your superheroes be

their mentor as teachers guide to true peace."
"We know that Ruler Zubbler, his crew escaped
and are hiding out on a planet attached to
Nimble just waiting to pounce back.

We looked at the video footage of Ruler
Zubbler as he sets in prison without bars for his
trial, digital electronic bounty kept him within
limited. A few loyal Sky Watchers felt sorry and
had forgiven the Pirates decided to help the
Chief escape late one night. They lower the
power bars on the cell and he followed the
rescuers down and around underground waste
systems. Most of the planet was asleep including
the gatekeepers, Neo was traveling the universe.
Monk, see you were back in New York playing
in Harlem nightclub. A couple of softie Sky
Watchers have breached security at the prison
with Zubbler." "Why someone did not alert the
gatekeepers or the guard's Monk ask Constar
Umar"? I figure it be best to contact you first,
not to bring shame to the planet since they think
security is much tighter now." Yes, you do have
a point, some of their own aliens are turning a
blind eye and helping this fool escape. The Orbs
lights flew high in the sky and went under the
wasteland, spotted Zubbler hiding. The guards

rose up in mid-air attacked with fierce blows to attack them. Their laser weapons bounced off the orbs as the Chief escaped with the Sky Watchers Guards.

Spiderman and Madam Butterfly made love hanging upside down in his bedroom, her large wings and long leg wrapped around him." They hung there half the night moaning and screaming in ecstasy, soon they floated back down to the bed as she moved slowly under him, and fell asleep.

Early that morning while they were still in bed, Constar Umar came into another dimension and talk to Madam Butterfly. "Why hello, Constar Umar she said what's up?" "See you've all been busy, anyway now before you can go all bring the escaped chief back to stand trial you will need orb lights to carry out this special mission." "So, he's on the run again, we have to make sure he is not trying to do a retake on Planet Nimble she stated," "We try to prevent that from happening, you all be fighting enemies along the way who dislike the orb lights. "They would try to destroy and defeat you all from reaching that planet to take them back for trials." "I will go over in another dimension to help and guide you all at a distance through the challenges you will fight in order to capture the Pirates." Up here in outer space, it's much easier to fight the hidden enemies, they are in the open." "Do not worry, I will have you all backs when the time comes." "Good, said Madam Butterfly, as she squirrels up to Spiderman in bed with her large wings over the bed, after she wore him out last night." He was sleeping like a baby, damn, I'm good she said to herself, like wearing out these superhero guys it gives me more pleasure."

The following week, the four went into Planet Nimble floating dense forest world to begin their challenges and were given the orb lights, attaching them to their waistbands. "Without uttering a word, instantly, they all transformed invisible, to see if the Sky-Watcher would accept their presence without another confrontation. Soon, they realize them as special friends who helped to rescue them from the Cosmic Pirates invaders. However, as they moved through the rough territory closer to a huge mountain hundreds of huge monsters with twelve large heads approached. "All their eyes were upon them, the four superheroes all stood still in midair pulsating in and out of dimensions, what are you going to do earth folks they all shouted?" "Monk reason with them that you meant no harm, urged Constar Umar." "Look stated Monk; do not want any trouble out of you fools, from what I heard you all are the entire smartness ones here."" No one ever told us that before the monsters uttered in beastly loud voices." "See, it takes somebody like us to see that in you, Superman said." The rest of the heads argue with each other saying they are better. Why they stood there arguing amongst themselves, they ease on toward the location of the old governor body ruler of the Nimble has to capture Ruler Zubbler. "You did good friends without fear said Constar Umar." "Your wits and quick thinking will save you from these want-to-be nosey creatures, now you all see what you are against." "I think you all can handle it from here on out my friends so the Space Aliens Federations have given you all the permission to continue.

They wander deep into the forest as it became pit dark as they saw other planets attached to Nimble." The Nimble's consider this location no man's land.  "So, that's why they place a guarded kingdom on this end, to be able to intercept any intruders from outer worlds. "They let the Pirates through to hide out, must be a connection Spiderman said." "I guess they want to feel independent and in control of their own destiny." "Now, I see they have many safer systems in place after what happened here a few months ago, stated Madam Butterfly." "Oh yes, there are thousands of planets that are attached to each other, some has less aliens Constar Umar said."

"Seem like the aliens back here are afraid of outsiders, maybe that's why they uses the monsters to stop intruders." "Most of them have been mutated by the Pirates invaders chemicals biological weapons." "No unity amongst them, some have twenty heads on one body who disagrees with each other all the time." "Monk Train, I figure if you can get on this planet have a one-man concert, interact and convince them to get along, and live-in peace. "Maybe, obtain the same measures with their leaders without my help who knows man give it a try said, Superman."

"You guys go take the orb lights and go meet your second challenges Constar Umar stated." After a few miles deep onto the planet, they came upon a very old creepy looking building. No one seems to live there, once inside switches on orb lights it lit up the entire interior. A few seconds went by, seemly out of thin air seven king's heads with crowns on one huge body spoke in echoing sound voices. Do not be afraid folks, we are not mutated, all of our staff have been affected and are scattered amongst the peasants of the land. As they, all stood staring at these kings wondering what they had gotten themselves into; the bright lights from the orbs illumined their faces. "We know all about the reasons you all are here, thanks to our good friend Neo."" So, you know him too, that kind of clear things up a bit said, Superman." "Therefore, you know we here to capture Ruler Zubbler them and bring them back for trial?" Yes, we know, as they pointed in fearful voices." Monk turned quickly gazing at a large group of mutated castle guards who has taken control. "Look he said, we can all be gentlemen and talk this through, everybody goes away happy." "What if we do not want to go away happy humans stated one of them?" "The rest roaring with laugher and chanting we will never surrender our friend Ruler Zubbler to anyone." The orb transformed Monk them into a gigantic twenty-headed creature, "now do we talk or take what I came for, the choice up to you all, he commanded." They stood back looking up at the fifty-foot-tall creatures; the four rose up in mid-air inside the castle. The guards attacked with fierce blows as Monk transformed into many shapes and solid forms. "Why they do not attack with weapons, the kings said to each other, maybe they trying to convince them that's not the way to go and wearing them thin too." "Ok, ok all the guards shouted you all win, this battle not going the way we normally fight and you have not killed any of us, we will let you have what you came for." They listened, but stayed suspended as a giant to make sure no changes of hearts and watch as each guard lay their weapons on the floor. Spiderman spurned his webs glue snatching up all the weapons quickly.

They notice five of the guards sneaked out through a side door with weapons intact. Gathering up all weapons and used the orb lights to deactivate them. Superman rushes outside to finish off the ones that escaped, as he soars over the castle scanning the areas with them nowhere in sight. Let me go back inside to check on the kings, make sure everything is back in order. Once the meeting was over at the castle, the four waved good-bye and flew on to meet their next challenge.

Monk Train realizing they could have stayed looking like a monster, plus no one would dare to mess with them, be their backup. They continued to fly without breaking a sweat, no sun insight on this planet, all trees gave off light. As the orb lights floated beside them, notices far ahead in the distance a large group standing in the open, maybe they the welcome crew or maybe not. Not wanting to take a chance, they headed in a different direction; suddenly a familiar voice spoke to him. "No, you must go face them and deal with it whatever it might be and you have the power to do it." "We tired from the battles sir, settling down by a large shaded tree not responding to the voice, knowing it was Congress Umar.

Thirty minutes later, they return to the same trail, headed straight toward where the strangers gathered. Upon arriving no one insight, feeling unease and glancing around at the strange-looking buildings. "Where all the people's Superman asked." "Earth folks over here if you looking for us, plus those little orb toys not going to be much help in this environment pal. As they turns and gazes behold it is the guards with thousands of backup warriors, all looking vicious. There stood Ruler Zubbler in their mist laughing very loud as a miniature sun floats above. "Ok, if you want me to come gets me you four Clowns if you dare and value your life." As the warriors advance toward him, they flew up converted into the giant monster, and grabbed their orb lights to save the day. The entire crowd laughed and cheered as they moved forward to take him down. The four stood in midair for a moment; soon they all lifted off the ground, and Monk Train started playing jazz on his saxophone. The fools begins to dance forgetting their mission to prevent Ruler Zubbler capture. As he stood on the ground alone and helpless, Spiderman snatched the overhead floating artificial sun and the Chief soon became weak

and falls to the ground. Madam Butterfly flew in, picked up Ruler Zubbler, and they all flew him back to Planet Nimble in a large golden shining cage. Few of his loyal guards were in tow behind him trying to bribe Superman, sorry friends he told them.

Ruler Zubbler and the Sky Watchers traitors were placed into separate cells in the center of the prison to be watched 24/7. Monk figures the trial is two days away, he just hangs around down here. Not caring for the women's here just not his type, until he met Regina who can transform into an earthly woman. That night, she made Monk forget being married and never to think that way again.

Day for Ruler Zubbler trial to be sentenced, the judge had spoken earlier to his councils and Monk. We find you guilty Chief for carrying out the deadliest crime against all on Planet Nimble citizens. He sets with a smirk look on his face, closes his eyes for a few seconds. "Judge, I have no place to go, he shouted out." Well, we have the perfect place for you, returning you back to your enemies on planet Jupiter they will be glad to have you back." Please, please I'll go anywhere else but not their Judge." "Well, you won't be alone, your Sky Watchers friends who feels sorry for you will go back with you, they protect you." Monk, they are yours now, get all them out of my sight the judge ordered." Thank you, sir, I will be glad to escort them to Jupiter, let us go fool and they boarded an old rocket ship that brought the Pirates to Nimble. Once the ship got into orbit around planet Jupiter and identify as a foe, they shoot it down. Superman looked over toward them smiled and they all flew back to earth that day.

A few months later, Dr. Delbert and few scientists came back to work with Nimble's scientists to experiment with futurist butterflies' clones. It was done for the future of the Nimble converting the upper part of their bodies all with wings being able to fly. Now, they would be able to go up through the portal exit into earth's dense forest on cloudy days and replenish their energy. If uninformed or human stalkers try to capture them, they will quickly fly back to their beloved planet below.

Groups still linking together giving out an array of earth-sun momentum to the Nimble up in the sky. The whole planet was back to its completeness, their body light energy was now lit up all over casting many deep shadows. Millions of them flew into the other planets with fierceness locating the prison planets that house the entire gatekeeper's forces and freed them.

Earth regime created international laws put into effect not to take any butterfly from that area. Stiff fines were imposed or five years in prison. It became a national treasure. To this day, an earth invasion was stopped by the Madam Butterfly, Monk Train, Superman, Spiderman, and Dr. Dilbert. Only private citizens that take an oath is granted permission to carry out peaceful scientific mission onto Nimble Star. Now, the earth regimes and elite space troopers knows about them, realizing they are not a national or international threat. To protect itself from all world news media they label the new species flying over the dense forest as (UFB) Unidentified Flying Butterflies. As you know the shadow regimes are not letting up, more advanced satellites, drones, and spies are in that area. Just for countermeasure defense in the case, the Nimble's Star leaders decides to become territory ambition a general told earth Leaders.

As the two suns settles in the west, millions of Nimble's with wings attached comes up out of the

Portal and settle on the huge tree's leaves energizing their bodies. They met earth butterflies, became close friends except for Mama Butterfly, she kept a distance to be on the safe side. She knew if the museums around the earth see her beautiful butterfly wings, they would want to put her on display, after all, she is a sexy lady first, and a superhero second. Standing there with her hair blowing in the wind.

The Nimble Aliens never went near any human huge populated area to see the tall buildings they heard about. Neo stood on a distant mountain hill with Professor Dilbert and the four Superheroes, gazing at the beautiful sight in the forest. "For now, we both have achieved a goal of unification amongst our different two worlds, Neo stated." "Looked up at Madam Butterfly winked and said Thanks, she smiles wave's goodbye with the rest of her friends." He raised up off the ground swiftly flew toward the Nimble Butterflies they flew back toward the portal hidden in the dense forest went back down to their home. "The elite earth space troopers' waves at them as they stood guard with missiles all over the forest looking up at the skies and the early warning space satellites eyeing the universe. Earth leaders never knew that the Space Pirates and Ruler Zubbler had been captured their days of terrors are over. Now, Planet Earth is at a crossroads to try peaceful solving it on critical problems like the aliens on Planet Nimble. Maybe they need Superheroes with true morals conscious to fight injustice and bring peace to Earth. Madam Butterfly climbed into her convertible sports car drove away from the forest thinking about her butterfly collection, should she release and set them free.

## About Author:

D. G. GUNTeR is a prolific author/illustrator that Specializes in writing Science Fiction, Urban Fiction, Space Aliens Technologies and Jazz Fantasy stories. He has been writing for over thirty years. GUNTeR lives in Newnan/Atlanta Georgia where he writes stories/compose Jazz instrumental music and does his paintings fulltime.